Born in 1944 in Tengaipattanam, a village in the erstwhile princely state of Travancore, Thoppil Mohammed Meeran drew inspiration from the sea and the fields, the rivers and hills surrounding his village. The Muslims of Meeran's village were, roughly, divided by their wealth and pedigree into two communities: prosperous Muslims who claimed an Arab, and hence superior, lineage and poorer Muslim peasants and labourers called the Thoppu. Meeran belongs to the latter community, who were treated with contempt and exploited by the land-owning prosperous Muslims, and the personae of his writings are people Meeran has known from his village, or heard of in the village lore.

Meeran writes in Tamil and most of his work—four novels and three short story collections—has been translated into several Indian languages, including English. The present book (titled *Oru Kadalora Kiramathin Kathai* in Tamil) was published by the author himself in 1988. Subsequently, it became prescribed reading in universities in Kerala and Tamil Nadu. His other novels are *Thuraimugam* (1991, *Harbour*), *Koonan Thoppu* (1993, *The Grove of A Hunchback*) and *Saivu Narkkali* (1995, *Easy Chair*). *Saivu Narkkali* was recently awarded the Kendriya Sahitya Akademi Award for 1997.

M. Vijayalakshmi works as Librarian at the Sahitya Akademi Library, New Delhi.

THOPPIL MOHAMMED MEERAN

The Story Of A Seaside Village

Translated by

M. Vijayalakshmi

Disha Books

Disha Books
An imprint of Orient Longman Limited

ORIENT LONGMAN LIMITED

Registered Office
3-6-272 Himayatnagar, Hyderabad 500 029 (A.P.), India

Other Offices
Bangalore/Bhopal/Bhubaneshwar/Calcutta/Chandigarh
Chennai/Ernakulam/Guwahati/Hyderabad/Jaipur
Lucknow/Mumbai/New Delhi/Patna

© Orient Longman Limited 1998

Series cover design format
© Orient Longman Limited 1995

ISBN 81 250 1544 2

Typeset by
OSDATA, Hyderabad 500 029

Printed in India at
Ram Graphics
Mumbai 400 022

Published by
Orient Longman Limited
Kamani Marg, Mumbai 400 001

Preface

I do not regard this as a novel. This is history—the history of an earlier generation. You may take it as a novel or as history. I have no objection to either.

None of the characters are alive today. They are dead and gone. I dedicate the book to their memory. You who live today will see in it your earlier generations. I hope you do not think that I am trying to find fault with them. That is not my intention at all.

We have not severed our connections with our earlier generations, just as the future generations will remain irrevocably linked to our generation and its diverse dimensions. Tomorrow's society may regard as strange what we follow at present as society's norms and observances. To them we may become objects of laughter and derision just as we feel today towards men of an earlier generation. They are our own ancestors. So let's not make fun of them.

I am indebted to Professor P. O. Jayarama Pandiyan of St Xavier's College, Palayan Kottai and Professor M. Khalil Ahmad of New College, Madras, to both of whom I am thankful.

I am also grateful to Janab Alur Jalal who encouraged me frequently when this novel was serialized in *Muslim Murasu*, to Messers Jalila Publishers and K. Mohammad Farooq of Sadakatullah College, Palayankottai.

KINSHIP TERMS

Machan : Cousin; Aunt's son
Mami : Aunt; usually refers to the wife of a maternal uncle; here, it is also used for the paternal aunt
Umma : Mother
Vappa : Father

1

It was around the time when the First World War had come to an end. A storm of immense fury and torrential rains destroyed the two-storeyed bungalow of Northern House Mudalali about that time. The Pechiparai bund overflowed and a number of corpses floated in the waters, bloated beyond recognition: a time the elders recall even today with trepidation.

Those were the days when Ahamadukannu Mudalali of Northern House was the chief trustee of the mosque and the village's most powerful voice. Someone complained to Mudalali that he had overheard the fifty-year-old Vappu, a labourer, address Mudalali's young nephew with a not-so-respectful "Come here." Vappu was sent for. He appeared before Mudalali shrinking in fear.

Mudalali ordered that he be given twenty-one cane strokes in the mosque after the midday congregation on Friday.

Vappu pleaded for mercy but to no avail. He was tied to the stone pillar that was used as a lamp stand and struck with a cane. As he was struck for the thirteenth time, Vappu fainted. A hand went up to deliver the fourteenth stroke. The onlookers watched helplessly, numb with fear.

"Enough," said Mudalali. He addressed the crowd. "If salt itself rots, can anything cure it?" The crowd stood mute.

It was a Friday of Rabi-ul-Aval, around nine in the night. The Kasargodu maulavi was about to begin his discourse. The mosque overflowed with people. Women huddled in the near-by school and outside it, in the unlit lane.

Mudalali sat inside the mosque resting his head against his hand. The maulavi seated himself on a platform. The mosque's modin walked towards Mudalali and stood silently to receive his formal order to begin the discourse. It was a strictly observed custom that none would address Mudalali till the latter himself spoke.

Mudalali took no notice of modin. The audience waited impatiently to hear the rest of the narrative about the prophet Yusuf that had in fact begun the previous day. The women had been swayed by the description of the prophet's grace and handsomeness and their number had increased substantially as the narrative was to be continued that evening. But they had to be patient and wait. For the mildest expression of discontent would be treated as an act of impertinence towards Mudalali.

"Tell him to begin," Mudalali commanded. The maulavi adjusted his topi and smoothed the folds of the Meccan shawl that adorned his shoulders. The assembly waited in rapt attention. The maulavi then got up and gave the audience a studied look. The hushed silence was pierced by his sustained chant of the first word of a long chapter from the Koran.

At that very moment, a horse-carriage drawn by a white horse stopped at the street corner. "That's the mosque," pointed out the man reclining inside. The horse was given a tug and it turned and trotted towards the mosque.

The gathering turned around to look, attracted by the sound of the tinkling bell around the horse's neck. The maulavi stopped chanting and focused his attention on the advancing carriage. So did Ahamadukannu Mudalali.

"Who is this irreverent character?" Mudalali got up and peered in the direction. The modin followed suit. Young boys jumped out of the hall to get a good view of the carriage.

A gentlemen, more or less six feet tall, with a forty-two inch chest and a sizeable belly got out. His Turkish topi had a red tassel. The rounded beard had a few grey streaks here and there. His black coat reached to well below the knees. Beneath it was a cotton shirt and cotton pajamas. The black polished shoes gleamed. One hand clutched a long stick with a silver handle and there was a palm-leaf fan in the other.

He removed a heavy box from the carriage. Fanning himself, he surveyed the surroundings.

"Who are you?" he asked modin.

"I am the modinar of the mosque."

"Pick up the box."

"Very well, but before that I have to tell Mudalali who you are."

"Which Mudalali?"

The modin placed a hand on his mouth and whispered in a low voice. "Ahamadukannu Mudalali. The Chief Trustee."

"We call ourselves Syedna Mohammadu Mustafa Imbichi Koya and we come from Muhalla Islands*."

The modin shook in fear as the stranger identified himself. He could hardly help running all the way towards Mudalali. "The Revered One has arrived from the Muhalla Islands."

Mudalali sprang to his feet instantly and walked out to meet him. The crowd, taking a cue from him, stood up. The maulavi got down from the platform. The gathering was told to disperse and the discourse postponed for the next day.

Soon, the modin appeared carrying the box, pursuing the illustrious visitor and Mudalali as they went inside the mosque. The two settled down on a rush mat. The revered visitor removed his topi and wiped the sweat, taking out a towelette from his coat pocket.

"How warm it is!"

"Ai, modin—fan the Revered One."

The modin carried out the order, fanning both of them.

The worthy visitor removed his coat and folded it into four. "You have heard of me, I hope?"

"No."

"I am the Revered Mohammadu Mustafa Imbichi Koya. I belong to the Muhalla Islands. Right now I am coming from Calicut." He

---

*Muhalla Islands are the Maldives.

took out his prayer beads. His lips moved silently as the beads slipped through the fingers, one by one.

"May I know the reason for the visit?"

"I'll come to that. Is the sea nearby?"

"Yes."

"And a river called Ananta Victoria Marthandam Canal?"

"Yes."

"Is there a mosque situated on top of a hillock on its bank?"

"Yes."

"Are there small hillocks to the south of this place?"

"Yes."

"Is there a dilapidated mosque there?"

"Yes."

"Is this the place which is hailed in old Arabic texts as the Abode of Faith, with mosques to the East and West and the sea to the South?"

"Yes."

"Which is the mosque constructed by Malik Ibnud-din*?"

"This very mosque, where we are now."

"Now I can tell you of my mission. A kafir jinn which follows the wrong path has escaped to these parts. I have come to seize it and stuff it into a flask."

"Subhanallah!" A hoarse cry emerged from Ahamadukannu Mudalali.

"O Martyrs of Badr**, save me," the modin screeched in fright. As he turned to look, he found the southern door wide open. The garden and the burial site with its sandal trees and prickly bushes and herds of unseen creatures frightened him to his very core. He quickly ran to shut the door.

"Ai, modin, why shut the door? Don't you see that the Revered One is sweating?"

---

* Leader of the first tabligh group, preachers, to arrive on the western coast of India from Arabia.

**The reference is to the historic Battle at Badr fought between the Prophet Mohammad with an army of three hundred against a much larger army.

"I am frightened."

The Revered One couldn't help laughing aloud.

"And how do you plan to be in your grave?"

Modin chose to remain silent.

"This jinn caused much trouble in Calicut. It would show the pious the wrong path, dirty the mosques. It would approach women in the guise of their husbands. While in Kannanur, I had heard of it. I went straightaway and caught it. I put it into a flask and had it lowered into the sea. It has somehow managed to get out and escape into these parts."

"You are right, Revered One. For the last two days I have seen someone as tall as a palm tree near the spot of the Lone Palm, early in the morning, on my way to the mosque. It was in white clothes. I quickly guessed what it might be and blew my breath on my chest after going over the Ayat ul-Kursi for five times. I walked forth quickly but it didn't follow me."

"It was a good thing that you didn't turn back. Or it would have given you one blow."

The fan sliped from modin's hand as he stood rooted to the ground.

"Ai modin, ai, you," Mudalali called out. Modin opened his eyes, wide with fear. His face was pale.

"What is it?"

"I feel strange . . . afraid. Someone's trying to throttle me."

"Sit down," the visitor ordered. Modin sat down, knees bent. The Revered One tilted his hand and blew his holy breath on the modin's face.

2

The school was housed in a hut to the north of the Big Mosque and was run by Hasanar Lebbai, the mosque's modin. Lebbai's duties were onerous. He had to call the faithful to prayer five times a day, fill up water, see to it that there was adequate water in the urinal and that it was clean, teach the children to read the Koran—the chores were endless.

More than a hundred children had to be taught and each of them had to be given a different lesson. Children starting at Aliph and going upto Aliph Lam Mim had to be attended to at one time. Lebbai would hear out each child and give an additional few lines to learn. Wrong pronunciation had to be corrected and doubts cleared. While going about his chore, modinar would fall into a deep sleep. He would then spring back to life when the children's shouting reached a crescendo. He would continue with two more lines and once more fall asleep. On occasion, one could see a streak of saliva trickling down onto his copy of the Koran. The children called him sleepy modin. In fact, they were hardly aware of Hasan Lebbai's actual name.

Ahamadukannu Mudalali had come to the mosque that day for the pre-dawn fajr prayers. There was no water in the tank. He put his hand inside but the water level was too way down to be felt. Mudalali had lost his temper at him.

The latter usually filled up the tank after the night-time isha prayer. But the modin had been invited that night to a moulood recitation, and a chicken was slaughtered after the moulood. He had completely forgotten to fill up the tank. He had in fact been late even for the early morning prayer call. He woke up in time, but as he was getting ready to leave, the escaped jinn came to his mind and his legs refused to budge. He decided to wait for company and reached the mosque late.

"Ai, modin! Either do your work properly or leave. For five coins, I can hire anybody in your place."

The modin remained silent. Were he to lose the job, there were a hundred others who would vie for it. And it spelled starvation for his family.

He began to fill the tank after the morning prayers. It was almost eight o'clock and the tank was yet to fill to the brim. Just as the sun was rising he had been to Pandaram's shop for a strong tea. Pandaram had arranged for modin to recite the Sura-e-Yasin on Monday and Friday evenings to attract his Muslim patrons. In return he gave the modin a free cup of black tea every morning, and on Monday and Friday nights, the tea was laced with milk.

Modin felt tired as the black tea was all that he had had since morning. The children had already started coming to the school. Their noise hit his ears like a drum ensemble.

"Elebbe, Maimoon has torn my book."

"Go away. I shall come and find out."

"Elebbe, Asiya called me baldy," a girl freshly tonsured, wept.

"Am coming. Go away."

Complaints, tears, screams, commotion. Modin could no longer afford to wait. He put his hand inside the water tank. The water was sufficient for the midday zohar prayers. He removed the rope and the bucket from the pulley and hid them behind the urinal. Were he to leave them about, someone would drop the bucket into the well and the well was sixty feet deep—one then had to search for a grapnel to take it out and that was no easy task. The modin tied his waist-cloth and put on his shirt. He fixed a white cap on his head and walked towards the school.

"Elebbe, Aidkurus wrote on the blackboard in Tamil."

"What?" The modinar's body trembled as though a most heinous sin had been committed. His eyes spewed fire. Dare anyone write the language of the kafir on the same board on which the Lord's very words are written?

"Who is he?" he shouted

Aidkurus stood helplessly in a corner, like a newly-hatched chick. A couple of boys pushed him forward, "Here he is."

"Come here, you pig."

"I didn't write."

"He did, upon my father, he did." The mob of children shouted in unison.

"Where is the cane?" The children handed over a long cane that was hung against the wall with a leather loop.

"Come here, you devil."

"What did you write on the board on which we write the Koran?"

"Lebbe, I didn't write."

"You ignorant fool." The modin gnashed his teeth.

The cane descended repeatedly on the boy's back and thighs and everywhere else. Aidkurus wriggled on the floor like a beaten snake.

"Allah! Vappa! I'll never write again."

The modin had worked himself into a frenzy. He wouldn't stop until the cane broke into two.

"Son of Satan." His rage was yet to spend itself and he wanted to continue hitting Aidkurus with his bare hands. He stopped with a warning that he might even kill him.

"Recite." He banged the floor with the broken cane. The children began their recitations.

The modin took off his cap and removed his shirt and hung it on a nail on the wall. His body was bathed in sweat. He ran his fingertips on the sides of his chest, slowly rubbed out little pellets of dirt and dropped them on the floor.

"Elebbe is rolling out pills," volunteered Aidkurus, who was still wailing away in a corner. The rest of the children burst into spontaneous laughter.

"Why do you laugh?" Modin rolled his eyes and struck the floor with his stick. Nobody laughed.

"Ele Maideen. Come here."

Maideen had long nails. Everyone knew why Lebbai called him. Maideen closed the book and got up.

"Scratch hard," Aidkurus exhorted quietly. He winked at him. "I'll pluck some tamarind for you." Maideen suddenly wisened up at the mention of tamarind.

The modin displayed his back. Maideen stood behind him and began scratching vigorously.

"Dig harder."

Maideen did so with all his might and the modin howled in pain.

"Elebbe, there is blood."

"Enough, go away."

"Mammadali. You come here."

Maideen could barely control his laughter as he made way for Mammadali.

"You seem to have no nails."

"No."

"Then get up and go."

"Who's got long nails?"

"I have," offered Aidkurus.

"You needn't scratch me."

Modinar now called Hasan. "Show me your fingers."

"That will do."

Hasan started scratching. "There's a lot of dirt."

"It's a mere twelve days since I had a bath. And there's so much dirt, so fast."

As Hasan went on scratching, Lebbai released a deep sigh and closed his eyes. He instantly surrendered himself to the spell of sleep. A streak of saliva soon made itself visible from one corner of the mouth.

"It's honey that flows from Elebbe's mouth. Gather it in your palms and drink it. Heaven will be yours," said Aidkurus and began

10   Meeran

his recitation loudly. Modinar opened his eyes, startled out of his sleep.

He rapped the stick on the floor. "Keep on."

He shut his eyes once more. Hasan was by now quite tired and his fingers moved on the modinar's back in a reluctant crawl. Presently, he too dozed off. His head lolled forward and hit the modin who was startled out of his sleep once again.

"Don't you sleep!" The modin rapped the stick one the floor. "Now, how many of you have memorized the lines?"

3

Syedna Mohammadu Mustafa Imbichi Koya the Revered One announced his decision to stay in the mosque.

Ahamadukannu Mudalali thought otherwise. A couple of months earlier a maulavi had come from Alleppey, much revered for his learning. The Western House Mudalali had got a room readied especially for him and made him stay for a month as a house guest. A chicken was slaughtered each day of his stay. A number of village notables visited the Western House to meet the learned maulavi and clear doubts on religious matters. Disputations took place on several points of the Shariah. While all this went on, the Western House Mudalali seated himself in the big indoor swing and enjoyed it all. A whole month quickly passed by as though focused into a mere hour. The maulavi departed, most reluctantly, upon hearing the news of his mother's demise. The one person who did not meet the maulavi in the Western House was Ahamadukannu Mudalali. An admiring crowd collected around Western House Mudalali after the evening prayer as he challenged openly, "Is there any other man in this village who can afford to slaughter a chicken a day for a whole month as I did?"

Fitna Maideen Adimai, the troublemaker, heard this and promptly carried the tale over to Mudalali's ears. The challenge boomed in his ears like a cannon ball and turned his head into a seething pit of fire. He could scarcely control himself and paced up and down, unable to sleep. He lit cheroot after cheroot and the butts lay strewn all around. Their acrid smell lingered in every nook and cranny of the house. His mind was in intense turmoil, as wave upon wave of uneasy thoughts hit him. He talked to none and hurled abuses at anyone who happened to cross his path.

When his wife asked him to come for dinner, he hurled insults at her. Viyattuma was frightened. The accounting clerk and the servant discussed it in hushed tones. Something was obviously wrong but none of them had a clue about it.

"The Western House fellow has to be given a telling reply that will make his head hang in shame. His family pride should be humbled, once and for all.

"This is the right moment. The Revered One from the Islands will be my house guest—not for a mere one month but two months. If necessary, even for three months. And there will be a continuous feast of fried chicken and mutton. The expense shouldn't bother me, whatever it may be—even if I have to sell of a couple of coconut groves. There will be roti—roti made with ghee. And ottappams. And everything else. Somehow our prestige should be restored."

Ahamadukannu Mudalali sent word for his accounting clerk Avukkar that very night. "Tomorrow is Saturday—go to the market and buy a few goats, chickens and some eggs. A Revered One has arrived from the Islands."

4

Anda hai
Mena hai
Anda hai
Mena hai

Ahamadukannu Mudalali was being borne in a palanquin and the noise could be heard from a distance. People moved aside, clearing the road for the palanquin. Those sitting in front of houses and outside shops stood up. Waist-cloths that had been folded up at the knee were quickly let down to the ankles. Those with their head-cloth tied around quickly unwound it and stuck it between side and forearm. People gathered in clusters to watch the promenade. Small children gaped from in front of the fisher-folk hutments. Their women peered from within. Those twisitng coir along the length of the street ran away to escape Mudalali's eyes.

Anda hai
Mena hai

The sound grew louder. The palanquin bearers slackened their steps while pitching their voices a notch higher.

Anda hai
Mena hai

The sound became yet louder.

"What is it?" Mudalali enquired from inside as he fanned himself with a fragrant khus fan.

"A cheeky fellow is urinating, sitting on the street."
"In the middle of the street?"
"No, towards the side."
"Caste?"
"Muslim."

At a distance from the path, Mahmood got up after easing himself. His right hand held a string of shark fins. He chose to completely ignore the shouts of the palanquin bearers. The onlookers stood awe-struck as Mahmood quickly made his way. It was almost midday. He had to have a quick bath and attend the Friday noon prayers. A few bystanders attempted to draw his attention, rolling their eyes in the direction of the palanquin that was behind him. His demeanour conveyed that there was enough space for the palanquin to pass.

Anda hai.

Mena hai.

The palanquin bearers were almost splitting their vocal chords. Mahmood still wouldn't make way.

"Go, and get that impertinent rascal here."

The palanquin bearers doubled their pace, this time not bothering to change their weight from one shoulder to the other. Their voices were almost a scream.

"Run and grab him," Mudalali roared. "Tell him to stop."

"Hey, you! Stop."

Mahmood stopped and turned back completely indifferent to the prescence of Mudalali.

"What is it?"

"Lower the palanquin," Mudalali ordered and opened the curtain.

"Who are you?"

"I am Mahmood. What do you want now? I am already late for the Friday congregation."

"Didn't you see my palanquin?"

"I heard the noise."

"Then why did you ease yourself on the roadside?"

"I needed to. I did. And why not?"

"Do you have to ease yourself that very moment when I happen to pass by?"

"I didn't exactly dirty your palanquin. What have things come to? Why shouldn't I ease myself, and that too in an unobtrusive corner?"

A strong stench arose from the shark fins held in Mahmood's hand. The palanquin bearers closed their noses with their hands and Ahamadukannu Mudalali did the same, using his silken shawl.

"Till now, none has dared talk back to me. Nor has anybody walked ahead of my palanquin."

"This street was laid out by the King and anybody can walk on it."

"And why can't you walk on the side, away from the middle of the road? There's enough space. You are an insolent man."

"Do you say that we haven't the freedom even to walk on a suitable road or to ease ourselves?"

"No," Mudalali shouted.

"It is this which is impertinence."

"What?"

"Haven't got time to talk. I'm already late for the prayers." Mahmood walked on without a backward glance. Ahamadukannu Mudalali's face turned into a blotch of red. His eyes became little pools of fire. His lips and tongue felt dry.

★ ★ ★

It was almost time for the Friday prayers. Hasan Lebbai began his call to the faithful. The mosque was particularly crowded as the Revered One from the Islands was going to join the congregation. Even Avu Pillai and Karuvai—the former never attended a Friday congregation and the latter avoided even Eid prayers—made it a point to be present.

As the minutes hand slowly fell to its left from its vertical position, the khateeb entered and sat on the pulpit. He was dressed in a silken shirt and an elaborately worked prayer cap, armed with a book for the sermon. It was five minutes past one. He glanced in the direction of modin. The latter got up and peered into the distance from the main gate. Mudalali had yet to arrive. Many of them had in the meanwhile got tired of waiting and had dozed off, slouching against wall and pillar. Those still awake and those reciting the Koran were impatiently glancing at the entrance. Mudalali was yet to be seen.

The Revered One Syedna Mohammadu Mustafa Imbichi Koya was offering the additional prayers before the prescribed one, yet to begin. People yawned away, one after another, in a chain reaction. Young boys kept up a continuous chatter.

"Elebbe, go and find out," the khateeb ordered modin.

"It's already half past one. Should we all be waiting for just one man? Begin the sermon," Mahmood spoke out in a tone of disgust. Suddenly the mosque fell silent. Each head turned to look at the man who had just spoken. Words that they had never heard earlier, words that smacked of insolence. But Mahmood sat with his composure intact.

"We needn't begin the sermon until Mudalali is here," someone else told Lebbai.

"We don't mind waiting even for two hours." Another voice joined the first one. "Those living to the east of the rock memorial have no right to express themselves here."

"The Malik Ibnuddin mosque isn't exactly a piece of dowry given in the marriage of women residing to the west of the memorial rock. It's God's abode. It belongs to everybody," Mahmood shot back.

The khateeb stood up and forbade the crowd to have arguments inside the mosque. Modin left for Mudalali's house. The door was shut. He knocked.

"Push it open." It was Mudalali's voice. Modinar did as told and went in. Mudalali had neither shaved nor bathed.

The barber could be seen sitting at the southern end of the verandah, sharpening the blade.

Modin almost shrivelled up as Mudalali threw a look of extreme anger at him—never before had he seen him looking so fierce and angry. He was tempted to step back.

"What do you want?"

Modinar's courage fled on hearing the harsh voice.

"What do you want?" It was now a roar.

Modin shook with fright. "It's quite late for the sermon."

"Oh!" The fact registered on Mudalali. "Today is Friday. I forgot even that."

He glanced at the wall clock which stood still, its pendulum motionless. "Isn't there anyone here to wind up the clock?" he was about to thunder, but didn't. It was an English clock brought all the way from Colombo. The day it was hung on the wall he had imposed a condition: "Nobody should lay a finger on this." Mudalali remembered his own injunction and swallowed his anger.

"Modin, is there a single being in this village who could choose to ignore the great Shakhul Hameedu Pillaikannu Mudalali and his son Kunju Ahamadu Pillaikannu Mudalali?"

"No."

"I suppose you are aware whose family it was that the Raja of Travancore chose to honour by sending the royal mare for a wedding."

"Yes. Your family."

"And do you know for whose wedding it was?"

"Yes. Our Mudalali's wedding."

"And the bride was from the family of Kunju Moosu Pillai who could dare to invite even the sea, mounted on the royal mare, no less. So far none has had the courage to talk back to me. But today, someone did."

"My God! Who was that?"

"It was that Mahmood, who trades in shark fins. How many groves does he own?"

"Can't be sure. Perhaps four or five."

"Which is the best among them?"

"Don't know."

"Go."

"The sermon?"

"Have it begun."

"How is your consent to be conveyed?"

"Ai, Farid," the Mudalali called out.

Farid appeared, his head clean-shaven, a blue kerchief on the nape of his neck.

"Tell your Mami to take a washed white shawl from the box."

Farid went into the inner quarters and came out with one. Mudalali wound it around his head into a turban. He carefully removed it and gave it to modin. The latter received it with utmost respect with both his hands and went down the steps. He began to walk towards the mosque.

Those assembled in the mosque saw the approaching modin, turban in hand. That turban, they knew, was equivalent to Mudalali's presence.

The modin came to the water tank to wash his feet before stepping into the mosque. At least eight men stepped forward eagerly to hold the turban. He who got an opportunity to hold it and keep it aloft till the modin finished washing his feet was lucky. The modin would however not part with it easily. He would do that only after he had adequately probed the supplicant's antecedents.

This time the modin gave the turban to Pir Mohammad. There was a reason for it. Hasanar Lebbai normally bought his fish in the last shop which was in the same row as Ahamadu Asan's chukku neer shop. As he was walking back one day, a fish of his choice impaled on a coconut frond's rib, Pir Mohammad called out to him from Ahamadu Asan's shop.

"Elebbe, I've something to tell."

The modin kept the fish near the cash box and came near Pir Mohammad.

"Wait." Pir Mohammad turned to the shop lad. "A single coffee and a tapioca wafer."

"Good. My throat is parched." Lebbai placed a hand as his throat.

"Then it will be a full glass of coffee."

Soon Hasan Lebbai had in front of him a steaming hot glass of coffee and a tapioca wafer on a plantain leaf strip. He slowly relished the wafer and enjoyed the coffee, blowing into the glass every now and then to cool the concoction.

"The wafer is good".

"One more wafer," ordered Pir Mohammad. Lebbai however didn't touch the second one. He asked for a piece of paper. A piece of paper was torn from the monthly *Al-Jihad* in which the second wafer was wrapped.

Pir Mohammad sat down next to Lebbai. "There's something I wish from you."

"You want me to recite the Yasin?"

"No."

Lebbai's face dimmed somewhat. "Spell it out. The fish will rot. I've to take it home quickly and have it cleaned."

"Henceforth I should be given the opportunity to hold Mudalali's turban or slippers, whenever they are sent to the mosque."

"That's somewhat difficult. Four or five others have already made the same request."

Pir Mohammad's fingers had dipped into his own shirt pocket and then into Lebbai's.

Presently, Lebbai took back the turban and walked toward the pulpit. People made way for him with utmost respect. The khateeb received the turban and placed it on the top of the pulpit, on which had been spread a green cloth. The sermon began at half past two.

"These are times when we pray even before turbans," Mahmood muttered, as if to himself. There was none who would hear him anyway.

5

The daily menu of chicken curry for two continuous weeks ended in the exalted Syedna Mohammadu Mustafa Imbichi Koya developing stomach trouble. He began to feel put off by the very sight of animal flesh.

The Revered One found himself frequenting the toilet almost through all the hours of the day. Ahamadukannu Mudalali's house had only one toilet. The women of the house found it particularly troublesome to find it almost always occupied by the Revered One.

Viyattuma could bear it no more. She decided to meet her husband to find a solution. Ahamadukannu Mudalali was relaxing in the Mirror Hall in his reclining chair, swinging his legs. He was looking into a deed left behind for him by Avukkar.

His head moved in the direction of the door leading to the inner chambers at the faint tinkle of anklets and the muted jangle of ornaments. The curtain moved just a little and Viyattuma became visible, her cheek bulging with betel leaves. Golden rings with tiny pendants adorned her ears along their entire shape. As she made sure that that there weren't any strangers around, Ahamadukannu shot a questioning glance at his wife. In a very low voice, which would not be audible to a second person, she unburdened herself before her husband.

"It's almost time for the afternoon prayers and the women of the house are yet to visit the toilet."

"Who prevents them?"

"The Revered One is in the latrine—day in and day out, all day long. What are we to do?"

"So what? We'll call the doctor."

It was then that Mudalali realized the women's plight. He recalled what the Revered One had said the previous night. "I don't feel too well. I seem unable to digest food. A dose of ginger juice may do me good."

Mudalali had himself crushed fresh ginger and extracted juice. But it was of no use at all. The Revered One didn't sleep a wink. The night lamp in his room kept burning with a bright flame, its wick having been pulled too long. All the water stored in the tank was exhausted. At the midnight hour, the Revered One had to draw water from the well himself.

"Couldn't the Revered One sleep in the mosque?" Viyattuma asked her husband, inwardly afraid of the very suggestion.

Mudalali quelled her with a fierce glance and she drew back, unable to withstand it. "What did you say? Do you know who he is? The Revered One is from the Islands, no less. His father was a seer capable of miracles. Don't you dare utter even a word more, or your mouth will be riddled with worms. Leave me at once," his voice rose up to a crescendo.

Mudalali decided to call on the guest. As he peered into his room through the half-open door he found his guest was gently running his hand over his belly.

"Let's have breakfast."

"I won't have any breakfast."

"No, you must have breakfast, at least a bite."

"I am not hungry in the least."

"At least touch the food with your fingers. If you don't eat, it will cast a slur on my status. You must feast with me for two months. And if you forsake food even but once, the entire village will hold me responsible. That will tarnish the image of my family."

The Revered One gave in before Mudalali's persistent pleading. He followed Mudalali and the two of them sat down for breakfast.

"I'd prefer to have fish rather than mutton for at least two days."

"Alright."

Mudalali settled down once more in the easy chair after breakfast. He called out to his servant Mastan.

"Go and fetch Avukkar. He should be in the store."

The store was in the southernmost part of the house near an open lot. Coconut and paddy were kept in it long with a mortar and a wooden pestle. Nearby was the roof under which the palanquin was kept. Avukkar was chatting away with Meenatchi whose task it was to dehusk the paddy. He did not like Mastan's intrusion.

"Mudalali wants you."

Avukkar walked quickly and soon stood before Mudalali, scratching his head.

"Mastan said I was wanted."

"The Revered One will have river mullet for lunch."

"It will be got."

"In case you don't find it, tell Abdulla to cast the net and catch some."

Avukkar went away to carry out the order. Mudalali crushed the burning tip of the cheroot on the floor. He opened the betel box, took out a shred of areca and put it into his mouth. He selected a betel and applied lime on it. He suddenly recalled Mahmood that instant. Such insolence!

"Wait. You'll be taught a lesson."

He folded the leaf and stashed it into his mouth. He spat into a spittoon that he had got himself all the way from Colombo, with a pattern of flowers painted on it.

"Faride," he called out.

Farid, who'd been standing near the well came running to his uncle, his waist-cloth tied properly and draping his legs. He stood respectfully before Mudalali.

"Did you find out if the Revered One needs anything?"

"I asked. He doesn't want anything."

"Nobody is to be permitted to call on him today."

"Yes."
"How many groves does Mahmood possess?"
"I wouldn't know."
"But you ought to know such things. Go now."
Farid turned back.
"Stop."
He stopped.
"Did you drink the water that was blessed by the Revered One?"
"No."
"Why so, may I know?"
Farid had no answer. He chewed at his nails.
"Don't do that and add to your imperfections. You must drink the blessed water and you'll be cleansed of all evil influences. You must get a piece of protective thread from the Revered One and tie it around your wrist. A kafir jinn has been prowling these parts. You ought to be more cautious. Alright, you may go now."

Farid was Mudalali's sister's son and her only child. Farid's mother, Noohu Pattuma, was the only daughter of Ahamadukannu's father, Shakhul Hameedukannu.

Noohu Pattuma's earlobes had been pierced in her fifth year by the family goldsmith, Vellayyan Achari. A specially fashioned pair of golden earrings, the like of which the village hadn't ever seen before, dangled from her ears. Sweets were prepared on the occasion and distributed in seven adjoining villages.

In her thirteenth year, Noohu Pattuma attained puberty. She had completed thirty chapters of the Koran and had read them over eight times. It was mandatory for all womenfolk to be able to recite the Badr lament, and the Muhiyuddin garland. Noohu Pattuma would call on Hasan Lebbai's mother everyday; the old lady was an expert at singing them.

It was she who first noticed the red spot in Noohu Pattuma's white garment. Immediately she sent word to Mudalali's house that their daughter had grown up.

Mudalali instantly called Meerasa the coachman. The horse was tied to the carriage and it stood in readiness for Noohu Pattuma's mother and two more ladies. Soon Meerasa raised the whip and the horse sped forward.

The carriage stopped in front of Hasan Lebbai's courtyard. Curious onlookers gathered on the road having caught a glimpse of Mudalali's carriage. Hasan Lebbai's mother fed Noohu Pattuma a little sesame oil and helped her into the carriage. By the time the carriage was back, the news had spread in all directions and the neighbourhood women had gathered in Mudalali's house. Everyone was eagerly awaiting the sound of hooves.

On the seventh day, Noohu Pattuma was given a ceremonial bath. The entire village was invited to partake of rice cooked in ghee.

From that day onwards Shakhul Hameedukannu Mudalali began to look out for a suitable groom for his grown-up daughter. He would lean back on an easy chair of woven cane while his clerk Vapu would sit close by, leaning against a pillar. Mudalali would bite into a cheroot even as he talked. His hand would hold a string of prayer beads. He almost never took off his heeled sandals.

"Vappu," he called presently. A whiff of smoke emerged from the cheroot.

"Yes."

"I suppose you know that the daughter has stepped into adulthood."

"I know."

"How about looking out for a suitable groom for her?"

"Yes, we should."

"Can you think of anyone equal to us in status?"

"None that I know of."

"None, anywhere near these regions?"

"I will have to look."

"Look."

"Certainly."

"Should be as pure as the purest gold."

"Certainly."

"With extensive property."

"Yes."

"It should be a family possessing elephants, horses and palanquins."

"Yes."

"The groom should have a status befitting one who will ride the mare belonging to the King."

"Yes. But it's a mere fifteen days since our child grew up."

"Vappu!"

"Yes."

"I have decided. The Northern House family never keeps a daughter for more than six months after she's grown. She has to be married off. Is it clear?"

"It is, Mudalali."

"Search. If it's necessary to have the marriage right here and now I am ready for it."

"Yes."

Mudalali made it a point to remind Vappu everyday.

★ ★ ★

That day Mudalali settled down as usual on the reclining chair with his regular post-lunch cheroot. He would be usually asleep before the cheroot finished. Once he was asleep he was to be disturbed by no one. Vappu arrived precisely at that hour.

"Where were you missing for the last two days?"

"Do bear with me, Mudalali, for leaving without informing you. I actually went to Puvaru."

"What for?"

"There's a well-known family in Puvaru. With elephants, horses, palanquins and extensive property. It stretches from the sea in the south to the mountains in the north."

"Good. What's the family's name?"

"The Punnavilagam family."

"I have heard of it."

"They have money dealings even with the Royal family."

"Excellent."

"I saw the boy. He is as bright as the fourteenth-day moon. A hundred eyes are needed to take in his beauty."

"Good . . . good. Did you negotiate?"

"Yes."

"Dowry?"

"To quote a price is beneath their standing."

"They needn't. We'll do more than what they may anticipate."

"They too have heard of our family. Hence their ready acceptance of our proposal."

"The Northern House is renowned in seven neighbouring towns, after all. You needn't be told that."

Thus was Noohu Pattuma's marriage finalized.

The day was fixed for the twelfth day of Shaban.

It was decided that the groom's side would feed the village and the invitees for seven days preceding the marriage. The bride's side was to follow suit from the day of the wedding for seven days.

The preparations got well under way. The groom's party crossed the river in one hundred and one boats. Two boats were joined together and gaily decorated specially for the groom. At precisely eight in the evening the boats touched the bank accompanied by drums and pipes. Prayers were offered in the riverside mosque. Men and women collected all along the route for a glimpse of the groom whose beauty was said to rival the fourteenth-day moon. A mare from the royal palace stood in readiness near the mosque. As soon as the groom mounted it, the sound of drums resounded in the air, punctuated by bursts of firecrackers. Professional singers sang the grooms' praises to the accompaniment of tambourines and cymbals.

The procession approached the bride's house. Ahamadukannu Mudalali went forth to welcome the groom, with a gold chain of twenty sovereigns to put around his neck. As he saw the groom's face for the first time, Ahamadukannu felt a shock. He was momentarily stunned.

A sixty-year-old groom for his one and only sister of a mere thirteen years? His eyes turned into little pools of water.

"Why do you weep?" The father asked the son. He soon understood what the matter was.

"Don't take it to heart. Are we ever going to find a matching family as good as this one? Their properties stretch from the sea in the south to the mountains in the north. Don't breakdown over this."

Thus came about the marriage of the all-in-all of the Punnavilagam family, Musaipillai Mudalali and Noohu Pattuma of Northern House.

It was the second day after the marriage. As he pounded betel leaf and nut in a tiny mortar and pestle, Mussaipillai announced to the village notables amidst whom he sat, "Actually I wanted this alliance for my third wife's second son. But he is only seventeen. I thought he should wait for at least for four or five years more. So I decided to be the groom myself."

The bud never bloomed. Instead, it was touched by blight. A sense of utter loss and devastation shook Noohu Pattuma. Musai Pillai Mudalali died when a boat carrying him capsized in the Poovaru estuary. She was six months pregnant then. Widowed in her fourteenth year, Noohu Pattuma expressed herself firmly against marrying a second time.

6

Sema Kannu Mudalali of the Western House rebuilt his old residence with its richly worked teakwood doors and shelves crafted by no less than the artisan who worked in the Royal Palace, as vouched by the very quality of workmanship. The top roof would itself have needed two thousand interwoven coconut fronds. Semakannu Mudalali's grandfather had decided to have a tiled roof. His own father had been about ten years old then and had some recollection of the occasion. The tiles had been laid, their grooves adjoining one another, and the ends were being plastered. Suddenly a tile feel loose and hit his grandfather on the head. Blood spurted out and his grandfather fainted.

A cot was brought on which he was shifted to Semakannu Mudalali's uncle's house. A cart was sent to fetch the famous Munjirai Chinnan Asan.

Chinnan Asan would treat only those who called on him. It was a rare occasion when he visited a patient to treat him. After a proper enquiry about the illness he would give a list of indigenous medicines and the method of imbibing them. He would also give tablets that had to be crushed into powder and swallowed. Such was his expertise that he could calculate to the precise second when a patient would breath his last. And it would happen exactly as he said.

The cart from the Western House halted in front of Asan's house. The driver was about to get down.

"Don't."

The driver looked up. Chinnan Asan was in a brief towel and massaging oil on his head.

"At what time did the tile fall on the head?"

The driver was dumbfounded—how did he come to know this fast?

"At eleven o'clock."

"Turn the cart around and go back."

The driver's looked questioningly.

"I needn't come. He is dead already."

The bullocks were prodded into a hasty trot. The cart crossed Pudukkadai, then Paingulam. The driver noticed a cart coming from the opposite direction.

"Where are you off to?"

"To announce the death of the old man of the Western House."

As the cart sped forward, Osan's thoughts turned to Chinnan Asan and his feat. How did he come to know? A Revered One from the Androth Islands had also made his calculations. He had opined that it was the devil that had aimed a tile at the old man's head. That it was going to take a few more lives.

"Can the Revered One suggest a way out?" He'd been asked.

"Of course, there are ways. We will have to prepare and sustain a fire-pit for two months and catch the devil with a help of a jinn and extort a promise from it. Then it will never come again."

This was duly performed. The devil was contained by a jinn. That day it manifested itself through the youthful Pathakutti, a construction worker. Patha Kutti swayed in a wanton manner, her hair flying wildly. The Revered One caught her by the hair.

"What's your name?"

"Asiya."

"What's your village?"

"Tenmalai."

"How did you get here?'

"I used to reside in a tree. It was hacked down to make a ceiling for this house. So I roamed around homeless. Then I reached here."

"What's your price for leaving us in peace?"

"The blood of three cocks."

"You'll have it. But how are we to know that you've left this place?"

"I shall wrench off a palm nut from the tree that's near the milestone and throw it down."

"Will you visit these parts again?"

"I won't."

"Do you promise?"

"Promise."

Semakannu Mudalali came to know of the story of his grandfather's death from an old woman of his family. He always nursed a secret fear of the house with its ceiling made of a tree that had housed a devil. He often thought of building a new house but was afraid of tearing down a lived-in house.

He then confided in a learned man who was there on a visit from Aleppey. The latter rubbed lime on a wooden board and drew black squares on it with charred rice powder, in each of which he inscribed occult Arabic words. He asked him to hang the board on the western corner of the house and assured him that he could start the demolition after the forty-first day.

On the forty-second day, the demolition began. The Western House was located on the main road behind the Northern House, at one end. The old roofs were dismantled and the walls demolished. A new foundation was laid. In the south-western corner of the excavated ground, a gold sovereign was placed on which the first brick was laid. The foundation-laying ceremony was performed by a Revered One belonging to the north who happened to be sojourning there.

Ahamadukannu lay in the relaxing chair, with its legs carved like an elephant's legs. He had lit a cheroot. A black cloud of smoke went up from its fiery tip and lingered on in rings.

Fitna Maideen Adimai made his appearance just then. He unwound his head-cloth, wiped the floor with it, and sat down.

"Have some." Mudalali pushed the betel-leaf container towards Fitna Maideen from near his chair.

Fitna Maideen Adimai took out a bit of leaf, applied a touch of lime to it, added a pinch of tobacco and placed the box back near the chair. He took out a size 14 knife and began shredding an areca nut.

"The Western House people are building a house."

"Where?"

"On the same site as the old one. A most Revered One from the north has laid the foundation stone."

Mudalali began stroking his belly. He did that whenever he was in deep thought.

"Why did they demolish the old house?"

"A devil is supposed to have lodged itself there. All that is mere talk. They are constructing a new house because they think too high of themselves. It's more like money that's making them do it. This Northern House too was constructed during the time of our Mudalali's grandfather. If Mudalali so wished, he too can have similar house with at least one of the three entrances that they're planning to have."

"Let him finish the construction. We'll see."

"People say the house will have two or three entrances."

Mudalali ran his hand over his belly. Each thought branched into another and yet another. What was it that prompted them to pull down that house? It wasn't all that old. And if it was meant to be a display of status, it needn't be directed at Ahamadukannu Pillai.

"Who's there?"

Mastan Meerasa came running.

"Call Avukkar."

Avukkar wasn't to be seen at his usual haunt, near the paddy-husking woman. He wasn't in the stable either. He was finally discovered at the goldsmith's, lighting a beedi with a live coal held between a pair of tongs that the latter used for drawing out fine gold wires.

"Mudalali wants you. I had to look in eighty different places before you could be found."

Avukkar stubbed off the lighted beedi and ran all the way to present himself before Mudalali. He stood, cringing with humility. But Mudalali did not deign to notice him. Avukkar tried to draw attention by clearing his throat. It was of no use. He removed the cloth wound around his head and wiped his face. Mudalali lay in his favourite chair, swinging his legs, stroking his belly. His eyes were transfixed on the ceiling. He looked like one lost in a desert, groping in vain to find a clue to guide him out. The cheroot turned gently between his lips to rid itself of the encrusting ash. A thin wisp of smoke rose from it.

Avukkar continued fidgeting with some more antics. His master looked up only when the cheroot singed his fingers.

"What do you want?"

"Mastan Meerasa said that my presence was required."

"Yes, I did ask for you . . . is it true that the Western House is to be pulled down and a new building constructed in its place?"

"It's true."

"Why didn't you inform me about it?"

"I thought you might know it already."

"In which direction does the entrance face?"

"It's behind our house."

"Then we should construct a toilet behind our house facing their entrance."

"Yes."

"The smell will go in the direction of their house."

"Yes."

"Arrange to get Kuttan Mistiri for the job."

"Yes."

It was time for the noon prayers. The Revered One came out of his room. Mudalali sat up.

"Why don't you rest?"

"I must pray."

"You could pray here, at home."

"It's been sometime since I prayed in the mosque."

"Then I would like to come too."

Mudalali put on a collarless half-shirt and tied a turban with its inner end hanging out stylishly. He put on strapped sandals and the two walked towards the mosque. People all along the way cowered back and gave way to the august personages.

As the two busied themselves in the prescribed ablutions, the prayer came to an end. Mudalali's face turned an angry red and his eyes grew fierce. He entered the mosque after the cleansing was over.

Imam Ali Musliyar was at that moment reciting a blessing. As soon as he saw Mudalali, he faltered and fear precluded any further utterances. The gathering now turned around to look for the cause.

It was Mudalali, with eyes like a tiger's. The very look demanded to know why the prayer had been carried out without waiting for him.

Ali Musliyar didn't complete the blessing. The gathering got up and moved away. Musliyar cowered near a wall. Hasanar Lebbai felt his very bones go stiff. He stuttered: "We didn't expect...."

"Quiet," the voice thundered. It echoed and re-echoed through the mosque a thousand-fold.

★ ★ ★

"Mudalali wants to see you."

Mahmood turned around.

"Yes, Lebbai?"

The words were repeated.

"What's the matter?" Mahmood was rubbing lime on sharkfins.

"I wouldn't know."

"Spell it out," Mahmood raised his voice to a harsh tone that left Lebbai momentarily stunned. So far Lebbai had not come across a man who would question Mudallai's orders. They would all run posthaste to the Northern House, discarding everything at hand. None had ever done what Mahmood was doing, and with not even a pretext of hesitation. A man residing to the south of the rock memorial. A man engaged in sharkfin trade. Impertinence was too mild a word for it!

"What's my reply to be?"

"That I don't have the time to come right now."

Lebbai shivered to hear it. The very words were blasphemous. His ears ought not to hear them. He plugged his ears with his fingers. The insolent fellow was plunging in with obviously no idea as to how deep the waters ran. He dared Mudalali, who could beat up anyone and even kill, if he so pleased.

"Are you quite aware that it is Ahamadukannu Mudalali who is calling you?"

"So what, even if it's the Diwan of Travancore who wants me? I have work. If I don't apply lime on the sharkfins now, they'll rot. And the loss will be mine, not that Mudalali's."

Lebbai once more shut his ears. "Allah! Not for my ears, such words." He walked out, his fingers still plugging his ears. Mahmood's wife was watching from an unobtrusive corner.

"It's the Northern House Mudalali that's called you, isn't it? Why not go and see him?"

"What for? Is he giving me my daily bread?"

"He is a Mudalali, a man of means. That's why."

"If he's well-off so much, the better for his wife and children."

"Suharamma has to be married off shortly. Isn't the presence of the khateeb and Lebbai necessary then? They'll never come without Mudalali's permission. Why are you so rigid?"

"The khateeb and Lebbai needn't be present if they've to come at his behest. Nor do I need his decree to carry out the sacrifice. It's me who's responsible for my daughter's marriage."

"Can you have a marriage with the whole village staying away?"

"It can be done."

"It is not prudent to buy trouble when you can avoid it."

"When he passed by in his palanquin, I didn't make way, like everybody else. That's why he wants me. And he'll impose a fine as soon as I reach there. You know what the fine is to be? I'll be told to make over to him a few trees belonging to me. He gathers wealth without the least physical effort for it. Why should we labour so much just to create wealth for him?" Mahmood rubbed off the lime that had stuck to his hands. He spread the lime-coated fins in the front yard. Immediately a swarm of flies descended on them.

"Bring me some rice kanji," Mahmood told his wife. He removed the head-cloth and wiped the sweat on his body. He leaned against a pillar as he muttered, "Ya Allah."

7

Soon the neighbouring villages came to know of the presence of a Revered One in Ahamadukannu's house and of his extraordinary gifts. Mammadu's boat, grounded all these days for lack of passengers, ferried to and fro once more. It was kept busy with repeated crossings, west to east, east to west. Mammadu charged eight kasu per head per crossing. Soon the cloth-fold in the which he kept his earnings was full. Women sat in the boat with veiled faces and umbrellas above their heads. Mammadu found himself a topi fashioned out of the sheath of an areca tree. To avert the eventuality of his waist-cloth getting unknotted, as he struggled to get the boat into the deep with a pole, he had tied around his waist a string made of twisted palm tree fibre.

Smoke spiralled up through the roof of Mammadu's hearth after many days. Neighborhood women smelt the aroma of curry leaves that made their mouths water. "It's all the doing of the Revered One," they said, as their hands intuitively went up to ensure that their heads weren't uncovered as they uttered the words.

Mondays and Fridays were crowded days—uncontrollably crowded, in fact. Requests poured in by the hundreds for sacred water blessed by the Revered One, for sacred threads with the protective armour of utterances muttered over them by him, for writing sacred verses on China plates, for the cure-all of his scared breath, for taming husbands who had abandoned wives—the list was never-ending.

The Revered One sat and slept on a wooden cot that was somewhat high, with pillows for the head and legs and a smaller cushion to plant his hand on, whenever he hoisted himself into a sitting position. A spittoon bought in Colombo was placed on the floor near the cot. The Revered One's left hand constantly moved beads on a string of prayer beads.

An elderly lady arrived with her thirty-five-year-old son. She got an audience with the Revered One after a three-day wait.

"He is the light of my eyes. He's my only son and all that I have to care for me in old age."

"What's the matter with him? Is he married?"

"No. All that he does is to constantly fight over rice and fish, like a child. He hits me as well."

"Is that what you do?"

The son laughed.

"What's your name?"

"Mohammad Mustafa." The old lady answered for the son.

"No. It's Muttappa."

"Do you hit your mother?"

"I don't," he grinned foolishly and hid himself behind his mother.

"It's the devil at work. I'll bless some water. Give it to him for three days. He'll be fine." The old woman handed over a container of water into which the Revered One blew his breath three times after muttering same verses. A spray of saliva accompanied it.

The old woman received the water reverentially, with both hands, on which floated the thin film of spit. She left the room cupping her hand over the mouth of the vessel to cover it. She stirred the floating foam with her forefinger and licked it. Placing a cloth on her son's head; she told him to drink it.

"He has spat into it and you want me to drink it?"

"Ah! Your mouth will rot, beware. The Revered One has extraordinary powers."

"Let Mother drink it then."

"Don't utter anything untoward. He will hear it. So great is he that he once made a roasted chicken fly."

"It flew?"

"Such is his might."

"Then he can make Mother a young lass of seventeen."

"Now shut your mouth."

"Then Mother can be married off."

"I'll give you a tight slap on the cheek."

"A new husband. A new husband."

"God. What do I do with him?" the old lady despaired.

"Faride!" Noohu Pattuma called out from the window that opened out from the room.

"Coming."

"Who's it?" The Revered One asked Farid.

"My mother."

"Fan the Revered One, Farid. It's very hot and humid."

The Revered One turned his head and had a fleeting glimpse of a fair woman in white clothes. Black curls fell across a fair forehead. Noohu Pattuma quickly went out of sight.

"May we be told the name?" The query was directed at Noohu Pattuma. There ensued silence.

Did an unknown male deserve to know her name? The husband had been dead and gone for twenty years. So far she had neither seen nor talked to any strange man. She had given up attending marriages and other ceremonies a long time ago. Her life had begun and halted at her thirteenth year. Twenty years of her life had passed like twenty centuries. Noohu Pattima stood biting her nails.

But the person who had asked to know her name was no ordinary soul. Perhaps he might mind her silence and mutter an untoward word. Noohu Pattuma feared its possible consequences. She peeped into the room through the window, quickly took in the hairy chest and the long thin nose. Her lips quivered, "Noohu Pattuma."

The Revered One turned towards the window. She went out of his view in an instant, giving him a only fleeting glimpse of black curls on a fair forehead.

"Farid. Give this cup of milk to the Revered One."

★ ★ ★

A mother and her daughter dropped in from a neighbouring village. They got an audience from the Revered One after a three-day wait.

Their village had no connecting road and they had walked a good four miles on a rough trail to the river to catch the boat. Mother and daughter left home while it was still dark, holding a flaming torch. As dawn broke they put it off, stubbing it on the ground. To avert the gaze of strange men, they opened their umbrellas.

By the time they were on the river bank the sun was quite hot. Standing unobtrusively near screwpine bushes, mother and daughter kept looking out for a boat and got into one as soon as it reached the bank. When the boat touched the opposite bank near the mosque, the noon prayer call was being sounded.

They waited patiently for three days to see the Revered One.

Ayesha, the mother, entered the room with Pattima the daughter.

The Revered One observed Pattima closely.

"Name?"

She felt too shy to utter her name.

"Say it clearly. It's the Revered One who's asking you."

"Pattima."

"Revered One," the mother began, "she has been married for fourteen years. She is yet to bear a child. At times she gets into a trance. Then she cries, all by herself. She keeps anything on her lap and cuddles it as though it were a baby."

"That will do. Some evil spirits are behind this, and I know the way out."

He gazed at Pattima's face. He took in the flushed cheeks, the quickened pace of her ample chest and the redness of her pouting lips. Her eyes were restless with unslaked thirst.

She stared back at the Revered One. Her expression was severe.

"Why do you stare this way?" She asked him.

"Do not say anything unbecoming to the Revered One."

"Indeed?" She laughed. She looked at him; eyes unblinking, lips slightly parted. Their eyes met. Seconds fluttered by as forbidden passions made themselves felt.

Pattima's mother stood, a mute and uncomprehending spectator.

Pattima's smile and look now exuded a strange attraction. Pearls lay in its depths, to be had for the asking. They were clearly visible to the Revered One. Those pearls had been formed by endless agitation—the agitation of youthful limbs held in bondage by timeless custom that would offer them no release.

"Don't worry. We will cure it," the Revered One told the mother. "You may wait outside for a while."

As she came out of the half-open door, it closed shut behind her.

"How long have you been married?"

"Fourteen years."

"Any children?"

"None."

"What does the husband do?"

"Nothing in particular. There's some ancestral property. He hacks off a few coconuts and lies about in the house, day in and day out."

"Does he love you?"

"What use is it even if he loves me?"

"I don't understand."

"I am the same, as I was in my parental house."

The Revered One stroked his beard. She stole a quick look at his hairy chest.

She bent her head, suddenly self-conscious. With her big toe she drew invisible rings on the floor. Her face was pink with a faint blush. Her lips seemed to bloom to a ripe redness as she touched them with the tip of her tongue nervously.

"Anyone there," the Revered One called out.

Farid came running before him. "Bring a long thread—a black thread."

It was brought. The Revered One wound it around his fingers and blessed it with a round of silent prayers.

Pattima was ordered to sit on the floor. One end of the thread was tied around her big toe. The other end was put out through the key-hole. Farid was told to hold it.

"Don't utter a word, whoever might ask you."

Farid nodded.

"I shall shut the door. I'll summon a jinn to control the spirit inside her. None should see what's happening. The thread will be used by the jinn to ride into the room and back."

The Revered One shut every window and finally the door. It became pitch dark inside the room. He struck a match and lit the lamp, dispelling the darkness. The Revered One then removed the string from Pattima's toe and tied it around a leg of the cot on which he sat. Pattima covered her face with both hands.

8

Rain poured down in torrents that night. A merciless wind uprooted coconut trees from the earth's bowels. The mud wall to the north of Ahamadu Asan's chukku neer shop collapsed. Ponds and wells overflowed. The level of the stream flowing by the cremation ground rose, carrying away the pot in which cow-dung fuel was kept. Frogs croaked noisily from the banks of the rivulets. Children moved stealthily to catch them with little nooses that were looped on the tips of pliant coconut frond ribs.

The washerman's stone was no longer visible and his donkey turned back, its load of dirty clothes unwashed. Children attending Hasanar Lebbai's school excused themselves pretending a desperate need to ease themselves. They soon arrived at the river bank and got engrossed in the frog-hunt. Some of them took off their waist cloth to use it as a net to round up fish. Hasanar Lebbai came upon them quietly. He administered stinging slaps on their thighs. "Shame on you, you are all bastards, no less."

The boys now grabbed their waist-cloth in their hands and ran all the way towards the school. The girls shut their eyes in shame.

The smelly village pond that was used to soak coconut fibres overflowed. The bathing quarters on the rivers could no longer be seen. People gathered on the river bank to see the swirling waters of the Valiyaru, the big river. A few brave ones got into the water to collect driftwood, bark and palm fronds. There was a rush to collect the plantains and tubers that had been cultivated on the breached river banks.

A woman's corpse was seen by some standing on a rock near the river mosque. Soon the brave ones wading in the waters rushed towards the bank. The corpse hit the rock and drifted to the southern shore of the river. Each had his own opinion about the body. The woman had been washed away by flash floods while bathing, said some. No, it was a case of murder and the body had been thrown into the river, said some others. Some were sure that it was a case of suicide caused by unrequited love.

The news of the corpse was duly conveyed to Northern House Mudalali who sent Avukkar posthaste to the village office in a spring-axle cart pulled by a Karachi bullock. But the village office was empty.

★ ★ ★

"Ayesha. A corpse has been found in the river," Farid told Ayesha, finding her alone in the corridor behind the kitchen. Ayesha was his cousin, Mudalali's daughter.

"You actually saw it, Machan?"

"I did."

Ayesha was the only person in that house to respect Farid and like him whole-heartedly.

Farid was a dimwit. Despite his twenty years, he remained a child. He ran errands for all and sundry and was not daunted by physical stress. He would pull water out of the deep well, clean the stinking drains, carry endless buckets of water to the toilets, even remove dung from the cattle-shed. All this he did without as much as a hint of a frown. Ayesha suffered silently and deeply at his plight; her eyes would brim with tears whenever she thought of Farid.

She could talk to neither her father nor her mother about him. Once she saw him cleaning the drains at her father's bidding. Unable to restrain herself, she ran to her aunt.

"Mami, couldn't you put an end to this?"

"He is doing you father's bidding. It's his fate. I have nothing to say."

Ayesha's eyes had watered and she wiped away the tears, hiding them from her Mami.

"Is it a woman's corpse or a man's?"

"A woman's."

"Old or young?"

"Young."

"Don't go to see the corpse. At night she'll come for anyone who sees her."

"Who?"

"My Machan."

"And so?"

"She'll then suck his life out."

"So what, if she did that? Why should you bother?"

"Why should I bother, indeed." Her face became a shade dark. "My cousin mustn't die. He should enjoy a long life."

"What for?"

"For my sake." She covered her face with both hands.

"For washing vessels during your marriage?"

"No, Machan."

"To draw out water?"

"No . . . no. . . ."

"Then why should I be blessed with a long life?"

"Doesn't Machan like me?"

"You are my uncle's daughter. How can I but like you?"

"How exactly do you like me?"

"You are fair. You have a beautiful smile."

"Had I been dark?"

"You are my uncle's daughter. I should like you even if you were dark."

"Do you like me only because I am your uncle's daughter?"

"Yes. I shall never see another woman's face or speak to one."

"Then why talk to me?"

"Because you are my cousin."

"Doesn't Machan have a special liking for me?"
"I did say so."
"I don't mean that kind of liking."
"What else, then?'
"Would you like to marry me?"
"Allah! That?"
"Yes."
"If uncle comes to know of it, he'll kill me.
"Why?"
"If he hears that I want to marry you. . . . He is already looking for a suitable match for you."
"What?" Ayesha's body shook.
"Yes, he will be a rich man. And I shall prepare the bath water when the marriage takes place."
"For whom?"
"For the new son-in-law."
"For my groom?"
"Yes, he'll be a rich man. He'll bring with him new clothes, soap and perfumed oil. Will you let me have a little perfumed oil?" Farid's hand roamed all over his clean-shaven head.

Little wavelets of longing arose in Ayesha's mind. She felt a deep sorrow for her guileless innocent Machan—an untainted soul. His face had the eager look of a boy's when he had asked her for perfumed oil.

Was it because of his lack of wits that Vappa was searching for a groom even though custom ordained that she marry her aunt's son? With a groom living right under the same roof, why look elsewhere? Machan had money, plenty of it, bequeathed to him when his father died. One needn't have more than that. Can one ever be married happily to someone whom one's heart didn't fancy? Whenever Mami related the sad story of her lone year of married existence, she had seen her eyes fill. "None of you should suffer my fate," she would say, gently stroking Ayesha's head. One could not but feel the pent-up emotions of a lonely life at those moments.

Machan was somewhat slow. There was nothing else wrong with him. He just needed some patient attention. And she'd give him that, she knew.

"Machan, marry me."

"Allah, your Vappa—he'll just finish me off."

"He won't. Machan should tell Mami that he desires Ayesha's hand in marriage. Mami will tell Vappa."

"Umma will hit me."

"She won't. Why such fear? Doesn't my Machan need to wed a wife?" Ayesha burst out out into peals of laughter. Her body shook.

"You look so sweet when you smile. Your teeth are like pearls."

★ ★ ★

It was customary for all government servants deputed to the area to call on Ahamadukannu Mudalali. They would be treated to tea by Mudalali. For high officials there would be a feast and a chicken would be beheaded that day. If a complaint reached the police, Mudalali would be first consulted on it. The warring parties would be summoned before Mudalali who would talk them into a settlement. Very few cases reached the law court.

Two policemen and the village headman came to the Northern house and presented themselves before Mudalali, seated in his favourite chair.

"The postmortem is over," the headman said.

"Is it a case of murder?"

"There is no evidence."

"Has the burial taken place?"

"Yes, on the sea shore."

"Buried deep enough, I hope, not to be dug out by dogs?"

"No. It has been buried very deep."

"How many groves does Mahmood own—Mahmood, son of Suleiman Pillai?"

"Six."

"Which six?"

"I do not remember."

"I want the details."

"I will write them down for you."

"What would you like to drink?"

"Anything?"

"Tea or green coconut?"

"I would prefer a green coconut."

Avukkar was sent to have them plucked.

"Mudalali, pray do not misunderstand me. It's Diwan Peshkar's orders."

"What it?"

"I feel hesitant to tell you. It's not fit to be told before your presence."

"Never mind, go on, tell."

"It's Diwan Peshkar's order that an English school should be set up in these parts."

"Audubillah! An Englees school!" The very earth gave way under Mudalali. His eyes forgot to blink. It was as though thunder had struck him on the head. Before his eyes danced the picture of burning hell-fire. The scorching flame and the snakes and scorpions fangs. "Should our offspring end up in hell for having to read in an Englees school?"

"It is a high-level order."

"We need not have one here."

"We already have order to find a place for it."

9

In the evening, a crowd of the petty shopkeepers would invariably collect in front of Ahamadu Asan's chukku neer shop. Urumi's cart, carrying its load from the market, would automatically halt at the shop. Beyond the shop there was sand and the carts' wheels couldn't move on it. Urumi's bullocks, their bones jutting out, had hardly the strength to pull the cart on sand. Their scum-ringed eyes secreted water. Blood was visible on their lacerated necks.

Usan Pillai usually sent his merchandise bought at the big bazaar in Urumi's cart. He would wait in the shop to collect the load that usually included whole bunches of banana, mangoes, jackfruit and similar stuff. He could hear the creaking of the cartwheel as it turned on a cobblestone. The wheels had not been greased for a long time and their creaking could be heard from a good distance. Usan Pillai got up and tied the cloth on his bald head.

The cart reached the shop. Usan Pillai unloaded his merchandise. He placed the crate containing mangoes and jackfuit on top of his head, held the banana bunch in his hand and walked southward. The petty shop was located on the way to the sea, on a piece of no-man's land.

The tinny contraption had been bought cheap and ferried across by paying one panam to Kadar Bawa. It stood on four stilts.

Usan Pillai was always the first to open shop and the last to close up. His shop alone opened on Fridays. He would sit in the shop and roll out beedis in a four-cornered palm-strip tray, his right thumb-nail grown quite long to aid him in the task.

Usan Pillai hardly slept at night. At twelve in the night he shut up the shop. With a hurricane lamp in his hand he would head towards the seashore to relieve himself. He would reach home at one o'clock and count the day's earnings. He would finally sleep around two o'clock and be up again before four in the morning.

The shop would open before the dawn prayers. Hasan Lebbai, on his way to the mosque, would buy a beedi from the shop. With that would be initiated the morning's business. A few would come in a hurry for emergency purchases of tea-leaves and sugar. That meant a quick profit of an extra two or three chakkarams per measure. Nobody bothered to visit Usan Pillai's shop during the afternoons, thanks to his raising prices by two or three chakkarams on any item that he sold. He stuck to the quoted price and never accepted sold goods back on any count. Someone wrote on one side of the shop with charcoal: "Fair Price Shop."

As usual Usan Pillai got up before the dawn prayers and walked towards the shop with broom and bucket in one hand and a lantern in the other. Hasan Lebbai saw him. "Why these?" he asked Usan Pillai, pointing to the bucket and broom.

Usan Pillai was too ashamed to respond. Lebbai was adamant.

"They dirty the shop."

"So you are off to wash it?"

"Yes."

"Who does it?"

"Bastards from near-by."

"Is this a daily thing?"

"Yes. It's a daily ritual carried out by the lowly scum."

"But Usan Pillai, you too should do a more fair-minded business."

"What's foul here?"

"All shops sell nettam banana for one chakkaram. You charge four."

"There is a reason for it. What others sell in one day, I sell in ten or fifteen days. Most of the fruit rots. So how do I make up the loss?"

Usan Pillai poured water on the lock and scrubbed it with a broom. He opened the shop, hung the lantern and lit it. The banana bunch was taken out and hung up next. And immediately, there was a rain of the over-ripe fruits on the cash box. The dried-up ends were now strung and hung separately. He lit one end of the thick rope-lighter for his beedi customers and put it in a rusty tin. He lit himself a beedi to ward off the chill and began to snip beedi leaves in the tray.

An agitated old woman soon presented herself. He peered at her through his old pair of spectacles that stayed on the nose with the aid of strings wound round his ears. "What do you want?"

"Have you got ginger?"

"Yes. What's the matter? You are quite early."

"The daughter has severe stomach pain. She is hardly able to bear it. Give me ginger for eight kasu. Be quick."

"There is a ginger shortage at the moment." Usan Pillai groped here and there and took out an old box. He broke a small piece off a larger one and gave it to the old woman. She gaped at the size of it. "Eight kasu for this?"

"There is no ginger available in the market."

The old woman walked away and after a few steps, halted. She turned back, stood, and cursed: "Let your entire arm break and rot. You are too greedy."

It was Hasanar Lebbai's habit to enjoy a spot of small talk at the "Fair Price Shop" with its owner on his way back from the mosque.

"Usan Pillai Kannu. Guess who dirties your lock?"

"I don't know Lebbie."

"Never mind. We'll do a little trick with an egg."

"How, when we don't know who it is?"

"There's a way. You'll need to wait at the seashore at night. Keep track of those who come to ease themselves and which way they go back. You follow the one who goes across your shop. The rest will be easy. You inform me and I'll put a spell into an egg. It will have to be placed in the south-western corner of his house. He won't be able to relieve himself and his stomach will swell up."

"And then?"

"He'll reach a stage when he'll be barely able to get up."

"He'll die?"

"He could. But that would be a sin, wouldn't it? Then we'll catch hold of the hen that laid it and recite suitable spells. Then the stomach will level off."

"It will involve much expense, I should think."

"Four to five rupees."

"Allah! Four to five rupees?"

"But of course. These things cost a bit."

"Let them continue to dirty the place. I'll wash it off. I don't mind."

Hassan Lebbai felt let down. He hit upon a fresh idea.

"Since it's for you, Usan Pillai Kannu, we could do for less."

"How much?"

"Three."

"No."

"Two."

"No."

"One."

"No."

"Seven chakkarams?"

"No."

"Four."

"So much?"

"Then? The tummy has to bloat."

"Will it?"

"Leave that to me."

"I'll catch the fellow this very night."

"One more thing."

"Yes, Lebbe?"

"The Day of Judgement is approaching."

"What?"

"This world is to end. Start your prayers."

"Tell me in detail, Lebbe."

"Take out a beedi." Lebbai was given a beedi.

"Do you know the indications for the coming of the Judgement Day?"

"No."

"The fact is that we are ruled by kafirs, infidels. That even men like Mudalali are being challenged. That Engilees is taught and learnt. That men have started to crop their hair."

"Engilees?"

"What else now? We are soon to have an Engilees school."

"Where?"

"Right here."

"All is lost."

"That's why I say this. It is the end of the world next."

"Should our children become infidels then?"

"They will die infidels. They won't read Allah's writ. They'll wear pants and walk about making harsh sounds like 'wot' and 'pot'."

"What's Engilees for rice, Lebbe?"

"Don't you know? Soor. In Tamil it's 'sor' and in Engilees, 'soor'. Instead of 'Assalamu alaikum' they say 'Gurd Marni'."

"Meaning?"

"His mother's chastity."

Usan Pillai laughed, displaying betel-stained teeth.

"Having a school. Indeed!" Lebbai gritted his teeth. "We should burn it down."

"Someone will show up as teacher, wearing a pairs of pants. I'll take care of him. One egg should do it. His stomach will swell. He will die."

"Sure we must. We can't spare the person who is turning us into infidels. We will get the reward deserved by martyrs should we kill him."

"Yes. A true Muslim must work against the infidel always. Only then is he a true Muslim."

"I agree."

"One more beedi."

Usan Pillai gave another beedi which Lebbai lit eagerly and walked away.

* * *

That night Usan Pillai closed shop early, surprising quite a few. He went straight to the seashore, lowered the lantern wick and hid himself in a cluster of coconut trees.

He observed each of those who came to relieve themselves and the paths they took on their way back. Kongannan Sultan came running at that moment. Usan Pillai immediately felt that this was his tormentor.

"I recall it now. We had gone to partake of the fatiha feast after Sali's death, in the village's Mosque-side quarter. In front of us—Kongannan Sultan, Dirty-Innard Peer, Dammu Mammoon and me—was a big china plate heaped with rice. When the first helping was served Mammoon transferred the entire plate onto a cloth. When the second round was served Dirty Innard packed it in his cloth. The third serving was grabbed by Kongannan. I protested. Kongannan swore that he'd take care of me.

"Is he settling scores now?

"Once he wanted to bum a beedi off me. I refused. He repeated the threat then too.

"Is that then the reason?

"Perhaps it is."

He observed Kongannan Sultan's path. He was going northward. He put off the lantern and followed him.

Sultan had a pole with him. Usan Pillai knew to what use it was being put. Presently Kongannan Sultan rubbed the pole-end onto the lock that hung on the shop door. He walked away, with total nonchalance.

"You are walking today for the last time. Tomorrow you will sleep an eternal sleep with a bloated tummy," Usan Pillai nodded grimly to himself. His heart felt lighter.

He stood, egg in hand, waiting for Hasan Lebbai. He hadn't slept at all. He also made a final count of the beedis given to Lebbai.

10

The evening sky was a calm blue with bits of cloud scattered here and there. The sun hid itself behind one of them as birds flew homewards. Fishermen stood in circles, repairing their nets and singing time-honoured songs near a cooler sea. Not a ripple was visible on the cool surface of the Valiyaru, which seemed to be listening to their music in devout absorption. All that one saw on its generous expanse was the silent wake left behind by Mammadu's gliding boat. Or perhaps it was a tell-tale sign of the Valiyaru's secret exultation with the music giving itself away.

Golden beams gleamed every now and then through the coconut fronds whenever the clouds gave way. The Arabian sea succumbed to the beauty of those golden shafts and lay enraptured.

A herd of ever-hopeful pigs and dogs kept straying before the fisherfolks' settlements who knew about every pulse-beat of the sea. Fishing boats and catamarans had been lying idle on the shore for a week now. Poverty was writ large in front of the huts. Children wailed out in hunger as women engaged themselves in noisy fights. Naked children roamed about listlessly. Their eyes were ringed with scum. Flies hovered around their bodies, full of sores.

Mahmood repeated his question at every door. "Does anyone have shark fins?"

"No." The reply was uniform. For a week now Mahmood had no work and no earnings. His family was being relentlessly ground up by the jaws of poverty. All that he possessed was a couple of trees that gave no earnings at all. If they could be sold, his daughter could be married off. A daughter who had grown tall enough to touch the roof.

Mahmood sweated despite the cool breeze. Perhaps the walking had tired him. He spread the gunny sack he'd been carrying on the sand, let down the lungi that had been folded at the knees and sat down. Waves came towards the shore and dashed their heads in agony, throwing up foam. Crabs got out of one hole and ran in search of another. The sad faces of the fisherfolk looked agonizingly at a sea that was determined to wrap up its entire body, ready to yield nothing. They licked their cracked lips, longing for a good draught of toddy.

Actually it was the season when the sea ought to yield in plenty. The breeze smelt of fish and the waters were calm. All the signals were right for a good haul, but even deep sea netting didn't fetch a single fish. Mahmood's relentless thinking led him nowhere. Could this be the handiwork of Mudalali? After all Mudalali was the sort who would willingly let his own son die, to settle scores with his daughter-in-law. Could he have used the Revered One's spells to prevent the sea from yielding—so that Mahmood's family starved? Will a Revered One stoop to such a step? Could he then be a man who valued fellow human beings? Would he willingly let blight settle on young faces and make a mockery of all values? Was he such a sinful man?

As the black tongue of night began to lick up the red hues, Mahmood's thoughts turned homewards.

The kerosene bottle with its chipped mouth would be empty. Rats would begin their nightly prowl. Mahmood got up to go.

The frontyard was dark. He threw the empty sack into the room. "Give me the bottle."

His wife handed him the bottle. "Modin came here before the evening prayers. You've to report to Mudalali."

She expected her husband to burst into familiar fury. He didn't. Nor did he throw her an angry look. He took the bottle and walked out, moaning to himself.

It was dark. The closest shop was Usan Pillai's. Farther away were better shops who charged less. But it meant too long a walk.

He could buy kerosene from Usan Pillai's shop and also find out why Mudalali wanted to see him. Usan Pillai might know if Mudalali was responsible for the sea's tight fist. If Mudalali was angry with him alone, why wreak vengeance on so many poor families, consigning them to the rubbish heap? Such enormous cruelty!

Usan Pillai was rolling out beedis in the miserly light of the smoke-coated lantern. He peered at Mahmood through his spectacles.

"Give me eight kasu worth kerosene."

"There is little kerosene available, thanks to the war." Usan Pillai poured two tinfuls of the precious oil into the bottle.

"Are you aware. . . ?" he began.

"Of what?"

"The Day of Judgement is close at hand."

"Wouldn't know."

"Where does the sun rise?"

"In the East."

"No, in the West. Now it rises in the West."

"Now, what's this that you want to say, Usan Pillai?"

"No, Usan Pillai hasn't turned mad. Do you know that we are going to have an Engilees school soon?"

"No."

"Then know it."

"So what if we have one here?"

"Are you out of your head? So what, you say? Our children will die infidels."

"It's alright, if they die so. Let the children learn a couple of alphabets. We are blind. Let their ears be open, unlike us."

"You have become hopelessly mad. You deserve a special poultice for your head."

"Yes, I am mad."

Mahmood didn't stop any further. He handed over the bottle to his wife and got ready to go out again.

"Where are you going now?"

"To him. To find out why he called."

"Don't answer him even if he provokes you."

"That's for me to decide."

It was pitch dark. As he walked questions rose before him one after another. Was he becoming a coward? Coward enough to go and see Mudalali? What if he didn't? And what would he do in that case? Perhaps anything—he'd do anything. Did he have the wherewithal to face him? Well, coward he wasn't. "We'll hear what he has to tell. And if I have to oppose, I'll do it, right there and then before his very presence.

"One needs to be honest enough to be blunt of speech. Let him resort to his wiles. We'll fight and die. Fight against injustice and die. We'll raise our voices against those who resort to vile deeds against humanity. Such was the character of our martyrs."

Mahmood reached the Northern House. At each of the four corners of the house burnt a no. 14 lantern. In the Mirror Hall a hanging lamp glowed bright.

Ahamadukannu was relaxing as usual in the easy chair. The crowd in front of the Revered One's room showed no signs of abating. Avukkar sat leaning against a pillar, close to the Mudalali. Mudalali had placed one leg on a chair opposite. Farid stood behind, fanning him.

"Who's there?" Mudalali said aloud.

"It's me."

"Are you without a name?"

"It's Mahmood."

"So it's only now that you came to know of the route to Northern House."

"I didn't have the need to know it earlier."

"You had been sent for, three or four times."

"I had no time."

"And if you hadn't had the time today, you wouldn't have come."

"That is so."

"Look here, Mahmood. In the entire neighborhood not a soul dares to talk back to me in the face. None, except you."

"They talk behind your back."

"Why do you protest at everything?"

"I believe in speaking out the truth, loud and clear."

"You can't oppose me."

"Don't a few oppose even God's Word?"

"I do not wish to prolong this talk."

"Let me know why I was called."

"Because you've to pay me a fine. You go against my orders, my wishes. If you are keen to reside here and use the services of the khateeb and Lebbai, if you want your neighbours' presence in your house for an occasion, you have to make out a deed in my favour. You will handover, till the last day of creation, the plantation of 30 cents area numbered 2319 in the survey, in my name. At the crack of dawn you will go the court tomorrow and place the deed in my hands."

Mahmood was silent.

"Say 'yes'. Don't be silent," prompted Avukkar.

"Get lost, you toe-licking donkey. My father earned that land through sweat and labour, not by leaning against an easy chair and swinging his legs. If you want my trees and the land, count and place before me exactly one thousand and one British rupees."

"You, Mahmood! Remember you are standing in the central courtyard of the Northern House. Even the Diwan Peshkar stands here with folded hands."

The Revered One entered the scene hearing the loud noises. He was in a half-sleeved vest, checked lungi and a green belt. Mudalali was somewhat put off by his unexpected appearance. How belittling that the Revered One might know that someone was openly challenging his might.

"Why the loud noises?"

"It was mere talk."

The Revered One got back to his room.

"So you won't make out the property in my name?"

"No."

"Let's see what you do when you need the village around you."

"For that I don't need your orders."

"Mahmood!" Avukkar shouted to caution him.

Everyone in the room turned around and looked.

Mahmood walked back in total darkness. He hit his hands together in intense anger. "Fine, indeed. My father's hard-earned land for a man who does nothing but swing his legs lying in a chair. He will consume it bit by bit in leisure. And we'll rot, cell by cell, in starvation. The Law of the Chief Trustee of the mosque?"

A small bird lay in a hunter's palm. The bird had to be saved. The hunter gave it the protection of his palm only to screw its head off when he pleased. He laughed because he could chew its young bones between his betel-stained teeth.

The school should start. A new generation should arise. Only then will man realize his own true nature.

A school had to come up here. Mahmood walked on, tearing through the night like a blade.

11

The night was cool and a pleasant breeze wafted through. A late moon cast silvery shadows on the courtyard as and when the coconut fronds gave way. Noohu Pattuma wasn't the least bit sleepy and she tossed and turned in her bed. She had been busy in the kitchen the whole day, yet, sleep eluded her. She got up and opened the window. The smell of the tethered goat that was being reared for the sacrifice assaulted her nose. She got up once more to shut the window but didn't. The animal's smell became tolerable now. She thought briefly of the goat with its dappled coat of black and white and its full-blooded youth. Her mind journeyed back to the night before her marriage.

That too had been a night of moonlight. One wondered why the beautiful dark had to be covered by a white veil. And lost in its rapture of the silver light, night was yielding in to day unknown to itself. Noohu Pattuma wanted that night to be followed by a night once more, with no interceding day. That the night be cloudless and clear.

The window in the western wall of the bridal chamber opened to an open courtyard which lay drenched in moonlight. Surma-lined eyes feasted on the moon's gift through a veil of fine gold lace. Young arms covered with golden bangles thrilled secretly to an imaginary touch and for that moment of bliss when the veil of gold lace would be gently removed from her face.

She could hear the sound of the door being closed. Her head was bent low, heavy with shyness. He must have not sat upon the cot. Let him come to me, hold my hand and make me lean against the cot, she thought. Her eyes were transfixed on the milky glow in the courtyard.

I shall look at you only if you hold me by the hand and look into my eyes, she vowed to herself. Seconds ticked away. They transformed into minutes.

Soon she heard the sound of loud snores. She looked through the golden veil. He lay there on his back, fast asleep.

The thousand blooms that had been drowning her all this while with their heady smell now seemed to have been cruelly wrenched, plucked and crushed under wanton feet. The moon's beauty fled somewhere and hid itself. This moon needn't have risen today. Why see it all, she thought.

She shut the window. She covered her face with her hands and sat in a corner. The sound of snoring boomed in her ears.

Noohu Pattuma got up once more and this time succeeded in shutting the windows. She walked towards Ayesha's room and adjusted the lampwick. The room was filled with light. Ayesha opened her eyes and sat up.

"Is it Mami?"

"Yes, it's me."

"You haven't slept."

"No, my child. Didn't you sleep?"

"No."

Noohu Pattuma observed her neice's face affectionately. She sat on her mat and stroked Ayesha's long tresses gently. Emotions choked her throat. Her own tresses had been even longer. She had combed them lovingly, nourished them with perfumed oil, as a young girl. For whose sake? To be felt by bony, shrivelled hands? For the pleasure of lightless eyes, that lay sunk within pits? Her once-silken tresses were now a sticky and unkempt mass. She hardly ever ran a comb through them.

"My daughter."

Ayesha looked into her aunt's eyes. Tears streaked down her cheeks which had all but lost their bloom.

"Mami."

"Daughter." Noohu Pattuma wiped her eyes.

"Mami, why are you crying?"

"You are seeing my tears only today. None but you has ever seen them till now."

"But tell me Mami, why do you weep?"

"Because I was born to weep. I tried my best not to, but I failed. When I saw you, your face and your hair, my eyes filled up. And to think that I am soon to lose you. I couldn't help breaking down."

"Mami, what are you saying now?"

"Your marriage has been fixed."

"What?" Ayesha was shocked.

"Yes. I was to marry a man whose beauty rivalled the fourteenth soon. I wept as I thought that your destiny may be similar."

Ayesha's eyes brimmed as she sobbed, "Mami."

"I realize it all. We are like domesticated animals, and mute as well. What freedom have we? We have to marry and mate even with a leper if it is so decreed. We are animals trained to be with tethered to mates and spoil more than one life. Don't you see me?"

"Mami."

"Daughter, I've seen it all. Farid is mad. Born to an old man and a fourteen-year-old girl. You are crazy to want him. The man destined for you belongs to a family owning three Arab horses. A family that once fed elephants with halwa. Farid is an utter fool. Don't encourage him. Forget him. His brain has meandered into the dark."

Noohu Pattuma went out of her niece's room. Ayesha lowered the wick. She gathered her hair into a bun and got up. She came to the window and gazed outside. She could make out Farid's figure, lying on a torn mat in the verandah. He was in deep sleep, lying on the side, hand in between his thighs. His clean-shaven head was visible in the moonlight.

"Suppose I call out to Machan? Suppose I elope this very night? Would Machan acquiesce? No. He lacks the maturity of mind for it." Did she have it? No, certainly not. She knew nothing of the world outside. Her own world began and ended in the kitchen of the Northern House, into which the sun never shone. Where to go, knowing neither road nor direction?

Did one need a relationship that the heart didn't seek? Why not end this existence by jumping into the pond or the well? On the third day, the bloated body would make itself visible. The police would come and cut it up. Then they would bury the body in a pit, like they would a dog. Rightly so, for this life is no better than a dog's. Machan had told her about the floating body of a woman who was cut up and then buried in the sea-shore. That had made her shiver and she didn't sleep for three days after that.

★ ★ ★

Farid threw his arms up in the air to shake off a lingering sleep and walked to the well. When he came back Ayesha's soft voice could be heard, "Machan, it's me."

"Why aren't you sleeping?"

"I can't."

"Are the mosquitoes bothering you?"

"No."

"Then why don't you sleep?"

"I simply can't sleep."

"I've to heat water by five o'clock for the Revered One."

"Machan, come here."

"Why, my girl?" Farid went closer.

"Shall we run away?"

"Where to?"

"Anywhere."

"What for?"

"To live. To live together."

"What's wrong with this place?"

"I am to be married off to a stranger."

"Yes. Into a family that owns Arab horses and eats off gold plates. Why don't you take me with you? I would love to see an Arab horse."

"Machan, I am frightened. Suppose an old man were to marry me?"

"So what? You can still have the Arab horse, watch the halwa-eating elephant and eat off gold plates."

"But...?"

Farid could see her eyes filling up.

"Girl, why weep?"

"Does Machan hate me?"

"Hate you? No, never."

Ayesha opened the door and stepped out. She went near Farid.

"Mama will murder us."

"Let him."

She caught hold of Farid's hand. Farid wanted to pull his hand free but didn't. He couldn't wrench himself free from that soft grip. The warmth of her touch was stirring new emotions in an unknown dimension of his heart. A fresh stream began to course through his veins. He looked into her eyes. They were black and intense with emotion. In those silent seconds of the night, Farid thrilled to the touch of this young woman in love with him. The thought revealed itself to him, soft as moonlight, that he was a man.

"Ayesha." His voice was heavy.

"Machan."

"How wonderful is your touch!"

She felt shy and let go of his hand.

"Do hold it once more."

"No." Her head was bowed down by shyness. Farid watched her face. She could feel the change in his look. His guileless face mirrored each of those new emotions that assailed him.

"Ayesha." He called as she ran back to her room. "I can sleep no more." He saw her lips parted in a smile through the window. Her teeth were like flawless white pearls. His heart was once more buffetted by a quick rush of emotion.

"Machan likes me?"

"Yes."

"Likes me how?"

"Likes you enough to want to hold your hands forever."

"Is that all?"

"No...." He gropped for a word. What to tell and how to tell it?

"Then?"

"Then . . . I want to hold you tight." Words tumbled out in a hurry.

Ayesha controlled her laughter with an effort and placed her hand on her mouth.

"Ayesha. You don't like me?"

"No, I like you."

"Spell out how."

"I won't."

"I'll no longer talk to you." He went back to where his mat was and lay down. Ayesha strained her eyes in that direction to see every movement in the dim light. Farid lay on the mat, all ears, in anticipation of Ayesha's voice.

12

"The coconut trader had rendered accounts."

"Did you check?"

"Yes. We owe him money."

"Is that so?"

"Yes. Ten thousand five hundred panams."

Ahamadukannu Mudalali leaned on his favourite chair. Gently stroking his belly, he decided that he would chew a betel leaf. He picked up a leaf and put a shreded areca nut on it. He put it back on the platter. His eyes looked towards the roof, at nothing in particular. He didn't speak for a while.

"How many panams do we get out of each haul?" Mudalali enquired of Avukkar.

"About five hundred odd panams worth of coconuts."

"Is this all that we earn?"

"The trees are yielding less because they haven't been manured at the root."

"And why weren't they manured?"

"I did remind you about it. But no orders were given to me."

Mudalali turned his head in the direction of Avukkar.

"I hope I won't be misunderstood. Ever since the Revered One came we have been spending twice the usual amount."

"Who exactly are you to bother about the reason for the expenses?"

"I merely ventured to speak on what I've observed."

"Which expenses have doubled?"

The clerk took out a piece of paper. "This month a total of six hundred twenty three panams and three-and-a-half chakkarams have been spent."

"Under what heads?"

"May I read out?"

"Read."

"Carried over to the first of the month chittirai is one hundred and twenty panams. Income from sale of coconuts, five hundred and six panams. Total, six hundred and twenty six panams. To Meenakshi, who winnows paddy, a wage of three panams. To clerk Avukkar, one panam. An expense of three hundred and one panams for buying river mullet for the exalted guest."

"What?"

"Yes, Mudalali, three hundred and one panams for his fish. Three big mullets were specially caught by casting a net in the Valiyaru on a day when there was no fishing. I wanted it for one panam. The fisherman was about to settle for it when the One-Eyed Jack from the Western House offered him a quarter panam more. I proposed one and a half panams. He hiked it to two. I said three. He now bid for three hundred. So I said three hundred and one. He turned back to go. Everyone there who had stopped to watch mocked him. 'Hey, One-Eyed Jack, why play around with the people of the Northern House. Even if it were to cost three thousand and one panams this fish will cook only in the Northern House kitchen.' The fellow looked as good as dead."

"Wonderful. From today your wage will be eight panams."

"Shall I proceed with the accounts?"

"No. We should straighten out our account with the coconut trader, at least during the coming two years, provided the trees yield." Mudalali placed one leg on a chair and swung the other. His hands began to stroke the belly. "I've been looking in all directions so that Ayeshamma can be properly married off. We may have to sell two coconut groves to have a proper marriage. Avukkar, who now has the money to buy our land?"

"Right now the Colombo traders have that kind of money."

"Ayesha's marriage should be celebrated in style, with a big enough kitchen to feed seven villages. She should be covered in gold from head to foot. Somehow we have to create the means."

"We will have to sell land."

"We'll do something. You may go."

Mudalali thought long and hard. It was a shame to have to sell a tree plantation to celebrate the marriage of the daughter. The Western House Mudalali would surely mock at him.

"What to do then?"

Ahamadukannu Mudalali couldn't sleep a wink. He smoked five cheroots, one after the other. How to sell the land quietly so that it didn't become public knowledge? No, that was impossible.

Every now and then a tin-box that had been left with him by Lakshmi, the money-lending widow, for safekeeping appeared and disappeared in his thoughts. Lakshmi, a short-statured woman who always wore white had given up wearing a blouse after her husband's death. She moved about freely, her gold ear-rings stretching her earlobes upto her shoulders. People pledged their gold to her for money. Her lips were stained a bright red. She chewed betel constantly and a bit of it always remained stashed in a corner of her mouth. She lived alone in a huge house set in the midst of trees on the bank of a rivulet.

Before a man could say his piece, she would overwhelm him with tales of her own abject poverty that deprived her of her meals for days together and reduced her to wearing her one sari day after day without a change. She could even coax a begger into offering her something, so the talk went.

Lakshmi lived all by herself. After sunset she would light the lamp in the niche by the door and shut all her doors and windows. They would be opened again only in the morning. She would shut her eyes tight and sleep, no matter who knocked at the door.

The only man she deemed worthy of trust in the entire village was the Northern House Mudalali whom she visited often. She was one of the privileged few who were admitted inside his house.

Mudalali would offer her a wooden seat and place the betal leaf container before her. He even offered her the spittoon.

It was dusk. Mudalali was getting ready for the pre-prayer ablutions when Lakshmi entered the Northern House from the back entrance. She saw Mudalali near the well.

"What's the matter?" He enquired of her.

"I came just to see Mudalali. There isn't much to be said." She then took out a small tin box that she had hidden in her sari and gave it to Mudalali. "Let no one know of this. Please return it when I want. I am scared to keep it at home. The dacoit Nakkan is around these parts, I am told."

Mudalali took the box and hid it inside a huge chest. None but he over opened that chest. The key was always on his person and at night he would slip it into the pillow cover. Mudalali now took the key and got up, holding a smokey lamp in his hand. He entered the room and opened the chest.

He took out Lakshmi's tin box, which had been secured with a small lock. A deft blow of the little mortar in which he pounded betel, and the lock gave away. As he opened the lid he could hardly believe his eyes. The box was full of gold jewellery and bundles of notes. He shut the box and put it back in the chest.

He came back and lay on the cot. His thoughts roamed over all kinds of terrains and in all possible directions, totally untethered. The head felt hotter and hotter. It might even burst, he felt.

The early morning prayer call could be heard. Mudalali thought he should ease himself. He came and stood by the well, holding the parapet. He continued to stand, hardly aware of the minutes slipping past.

"Uncle, shall I draw out water?"

It was Farid. He turned back. "No."

He went back and sat on the cot. "Farid."

Farid was before him in a trice.

"Call Avukkar."

Avukkar found his master in the familiar elephant-leg easy chair. He noticed Mudalali's muddied-looking blood-shot eyes. He hadn't even cleaned his teeth. He was silent though he'd seen Avukkar.

Mudalali got up from the chair and began to pace back and forth, hands locked together behind his back. Avukkar could glean nothing. Mudalali's actions were very strange this morning. Had someone cast a spell on Mudalali? Or perhaps some of Mudalali's devices against someone had hit back on the perpetrator himself! Avukkar craned his neck in the direction of the Revered One's room. It was still closed.

"Avukkare."

"Yes."

Silence, once more.

"Avukkare."

"Yes."

"Tell Karuppan to see me."

"I shall."

"No, don't."

A few minutes slipped by. Mudalali voiced his earlier order: "Bring Karuppan to me."

As Avukkar made for the exit, Mudalali called him once more.

"Avukkar, you needn't do that." A little later he changed his mind and Avukkar set off once more.

At noon, Karuppan reported before Mudalali. Karuppan was tall, dark and strongly built; he wore nothing but a brief cloth around his waist. Mudalali got up and walked through the open area behind the house. Karuppan followed, close behind. The two stood all by themselves near a mango tree. Mudalali whispered a few words into Karuppan's ears. The secret wasn't audible even to the breeze that wafted along the tree's branches.

That night Karuppan crouched stealthily near Lakshmi's house as the day darkened. An incessant rain poured from the skies and drowned every sound of Lakshmi's bones around her throat as they were crushed and powdered by Karuppan's powerful grip. The rivulet roaring by with the swirling flood waters received her dead body. On the third day a bloated, mutilated, fish-nibbled and totally unrecognizable corpse rose upon the surface of the rivulet. It floated along and joined the Valiyaru, rising up and falling down with its waves, and moved with it toward the sea. It was sighted by a few from the rocky bank of the Valiyaru.

"Lakshmi seems to have disappeared. Nakkan the dacoit has probably carried her off." Thus went the village whisper-campaign. Avukkar carried the same tale to Mudalali who evinced but a desultory interest in the story.

13

The shadows cast by the sun had begun to grow shorter. Jabbar the barber made his appearance before Ahamadukannu Mudalali, who had been impatiently waiting for a shave. Mudalali gave Jabbar an intimidating look. Jabbar cringed like a worm.

"When did I send for you?"

"A while ago."

"Then why are you late?"

"Today was the fortieth day celebration of Mahmood Kaka's daughter's child. They sacrificed a goat and had the child's head tonsured. I got delayed there, Mudalali, please forgive me."

"Chi, you ass." Mudalali's eyes were like two pools of fire. Flames leapt out of them singeing Jabbar. It was as though his insides would melt away in that blaze. "If you are so keen to attend the tonsure ceremony of a child whose house is to the east of the Rock Memorial and make Ahamadu Kannu Mudalali of Northern House wait for his shave, you no longer need appear at the doorstep of this house. Why don't you become a house servant of Mahmood's?"

"My precious Lord. My children will starve. Please forgive me."

"Forgive?"

"I went there in the hope of a couple of pieces of meat. You must pardon me."

"Impossible."

"Please. I went there at the behest of my children. But for Mudalali's grace, my family would be starving. You must forgive me this once." Tears were ready to tumble down from Jabbar's eyes.

"You will no longer enter Mahmood's doorstep for any work. Not without my permission."

"Yes."

"You may come in."

The two then sat facing each other in the southern verandah. Jabbar opened his tin box and spread a white cloth enveloping Mudalali's legs and his. He sharpened the glimmering blade on a black whetstone and wiped the knife on a piece of thick tarpaulin that he kept on his right thigh. He began his chatter, rubbing water on Mudalali's face; "Yesterday I went to attend on Western House Mudalali. The moment I entered I was given a big China bowl of tea, boiled thick in the freshest milk. Khadija Umma of Western House is a kind-hearted lady, a veritable goddess of wealth. The moment she notices my lowly presence, she immediately sends a bowl of tea. Or a meal, served with a generous heart. She never lets me off without giving something."

"It's almost noon. The hot water will become tepid. Hurry, I have to have my bath."

"I shall finish right away." Jabbar began to clean the stubble with the blade. He began once more, with an accompanying spray of saliva: "I enquired whether they had got their daughter Pattumuttu Suhrabibikannu engaged. I was told that they would do so, soon after they perform the milk-boiling ceremony, once they complete the house. I asked why not engage their daughter with Farid Pillaikannu Mudalali, nephew of Northern House Mudalali. My daughter wasn't brought up to be given to him in marriage, he retorted. How come he spoke like that?"

"The Western House belongs to the new rich, unlike the Northern House that belongs to a tradition with hereditary entitlements. We aren't so low as to take a bride from his side."

"That's true, undoubtedly so. Can there ever be a comparison between our family and theirs. They wonder why the Northern

House is on the lookout for a groom when the right match is available under their very roof. I didn't offer a comment."

The sound of a horse-drawn cart was heard from the main entrance. Jabbar wiped the blade between his fingers and folded it.

"There's someone here."

"You needn't bother. Are you finished?"

"Yes."

Mudalali came to the Mirror Hall where the tehsildar and the village official awaited him, seated in cane chairs. Mudalali accepted their greetings and sat down on a chair.

"What's the occasion?"

"We have something to talk over with you."

"Kindly hurry up. I am yet to have my bath and the water won't stay hot much longer. If I delay any more I shall catch a cold."

The village official rolled out a sketch and put his finger on a spot. "Mudalali has to give the government this piece of land to construct a school."

"For constructing a school?"

"Yes."

"Which land?"

"It belongs to Mudalali. It's on the main road leading to the shore. Survey Number 2320. Forty cents of land."

"We are Muslims. It's forbidden for us to learn Englees."

"What's wrong in Muslims learning English?"

"Because it will lead us to the hell which we call jahannum."

"Did Jinnah Sahib not learn English on a foreign shore?"

"He is an infidel."

"Diwan Peshkar has sent orders to acquire land."

"My land?"

"Who else can we possibly approach when it comes to help? We thought Mudalali will help us. So we prepared a sketch of his land."

"I told you that day itself—we do not need an Englees school."

"You did say so."

"I do not wish to give my land for such a school that will despatch me to hell, as an infidel."

"Then let Mudalali try to get us some other piece of land for the school."

"We simply do not need an Englees school. Nor have we any land to spare." Mudalali got up. "I must go for my bath." He walked towards the well. The village official and the tehsildar came out and got into the horse cart. The hooves dug into the sand and threw it all around. The cart soon crossed the turning that led to the Big Mosque and crossed the bridge. It sped fast and was approaching the mast-wood clump near Asan's coffee shop.

Mahmood was sitting on a short bench in front of the shop. The speed with which the cart came back foretold that the going had not been smooth. The cart had returned a little too soon after the onward journey. Normally the officials were received very properly, but quite obviously it hadn't been that way today. Mudalali would have refused to part with his land. Hence the speedy return of the cart.

Mahmood walked to the middle of the road and stretched out an arm. The cart stopped. He crossed his forearms across the chest and approached the cart. "My Masters," he began.

"What is it, Sayibu?"

Mahmood ran his fingers through his hair. "We are blind men. Let our offspring not be blind, like us. You must build a school for us here."

The man they beheld was in a waist-cloth, with a brief cloth on one shoulder. The face screamed aloud his poverty. He was in need of a hair cut and a shave. The black leather belt had turned white in patches.

"Your name?"

"Mahmoodu Pillai."

"Profession?"

"I buy shark fins on the sea shore and sell them for a livelihood."

"We couldn't obtain the land to build the school."

"Land?"

"It is Diwan Peshkar's orders that we should build the school provided we get some land."

"I'll give it."

"Where?"

"I have a piece of land near the main road—Survey No. 2319. I had meant to give it away to my daughter as dowry."

"We can have the school built if you make it over to us."

"I shall make it over—right away. You can take my thumb impression on that piece of paper."

"Your father's name?"

"Suleiman Pillai."

"Yours?"

"Mahmoodu Pillai."

"Age?"

"Forty-six."

"House name?"

"It is the new house of the palm-tree garden."

"Come tomorrow to the camp and give us your thumb impression."

"I shall. At what time?"

"At eleven."

The driver gave a tug at the leash. The horse sprang forward.

Mahmood hardly slept that night. He hadn't yet told his wife of his decision to give his land for the school. She would argue with him about it. But it was not proper to keep her in the dark.

He had no more than the thirty cents of land to give as dowry to his daughter. What would be left was a barren land that returned nothing. None would come forward to buy it.

It was midnight and Mahmood heard the distant crowing of the night fowl. He sat up on the mat and lit a beedi. His wife was fast asleep, lying on her side.

"Patta, my precious," he called. It was necessary to start for the village office early in the morning, for it was at some distance. One had to walk a dusty trail, starting before the sun became sharp, to make it in time.

He could tell her early in the morning. But she might shout and attract the neighbours' attention. This was the right moment to explain to her properly, gently.

"Patta, my precious."

"Umm."

"Wake up."

"Doesn't even let me lie down in peace," she muttered.

"Wash your face."

"Has the sky become white?"

"No."

"Then why wake me?"

"I want to tell you something."

"At the midnight hour? I won't oblige you."

"Didn't I tell you to wash your face?"

Mahmood smoked several beedis in quick sucession.

She came back, having washed her face.

"I have to tell you something."

"Couldn't it have waited till day-break?"

"Early morning I have to go somewhere."

"Why?"

"That's what I have to tell you. So that you don't remain unaware. I am going to make over to the government our land near the bridge, to construct the school."

"And what happens to our daughter?"

Mahmood was silent.

"How do you propose to marry her off?"

"More important than her marriage is to promote the cause of learning. Do they not say that our Prophet wanted men to pursue knowledge even if it meant travelling all the way to China? It will be counted in our good deeds if we give the land."

"We don't need to perform such a good deed. Let Mudalali give up his land."

"Who Mudalali and what Mudalali? Is he not a Mudalali who has amassed property by grabbing it unlawfully? Who sells coconuts that aren't his and fattens his belly? Such men are dacoits who do not use a gun."

"Then what of my daughter?"

"God will show a way." Mahmood stretched himself on the mat. He lay, ears sharpened, to hear the first crow of the cock.

14

Semakannu Mudalali passed away quite suddenly in the new house that had been completed not so long ago. The burial took place in the evening. Ahamadukannu Mudalali duly followed the mourning procession which dispersed after offering special prayers for the departed soul. Ahamadu Kannu Mudalali settled down on a rush mat in the hall adjacent to the mosque. It was his habit to spend an extra hour there whenever he went to the mosque to pray. He could thus keep track of the regular and the not-so-regular devotees and keep in touch with the village happenings. If one approached Mudalali for any help, he would first see the person's forehead—whether or not it bore a discoloured patch of skin that gave witness to the person's prayer habits.

"A person who doesn't pray regularly needn't come up the steps of the Northern House," he would proclaim. A prospective supplicant would take care to pray regularly for two or three weeks before facing Mudalali. Some would rub the forehead against the ground to achieve the desired effect.

At a distance, Hasan Lebbai was picking off lizard droppings from mats with small bits of paper and throwing them out.

"Elebbe."

"Yes?"

"What keeps you busy there?"

"There are lizard droppings on the mat."

"Come here, I say."

Hasan Lebbai threw the paper into the street and washed his hands at the tank. Drying his hands on the waist-cloth, he appeared before Mudalali.

"Doesn't Mahmood come to pray these days?"

"He's an 'eighth day-er'."

"I don't understand."

"Attends only the Friday congregation."

"Didn't he attend the funeral prayers?"

"No."

"Without my permission, you will not visit his house to recite the Yasin or the Moulood."

Lebbai was silent.

"Why don't you talk?"

"Of course. I won't go there. We are soon to be visited by the dark forces of misfortune and bad spirits."

"What?"

"We'll be shortly having Englees here."

"I say I just don't follow you."

"An infidel school is coming up."

"How now, when I haven't given any land?"

"Mudalali didn't! But there are others."

"And who dares to do so, when I refuse?"

"Mahmood."

Mudalali could hardly believe his ears. "He gave land?"

"He has given his land which is near Mudalali's grove as a gift to construct the school."

"And how did Lebbai get to know this?"

"From Mahmood himself, when I saw him in front of Usan Pillai's shop. He also showed off his left thumb with its coat of ink."

"So there's to be here an infidel's school... a school that's coming up without my knowledge or permission."

"That's right."

"He opposes me tooth and nail."

"He does."

"I shall break that very thumb." The eyes were already an angry red. "I shall have him bound to the pillar and flayed in the Friday congregation."

Mudalali slid his feet into his slippers and walked out, the slippers making a loud sound. Hasan Lebbai was wont to follow Mudalali till he reached his house. By the time he slipped on his shirt with its tiny blotches of blood caused by smothered bedbugs, Mudalali had got out of the mosque and hastened towards the Northern House. Lebbai ran after him but in vain.

Mudalali went straight into the Revered One's room, who was about to blow his holy breath into a bowl of water. He quickly put down the bowl.

"I've something to tell you."

The Revered One told the crowd in his room to leave them alone.

"Yes, what is it?"

"It's something very important."

"For everything there is a solution."

"Does our religion permit us to read Englees? Isn't that a sin?"

"It is a gross sin."

"If an Englees-teaching school is set up here?"

"It's an even bigger sin."

"And the man who allots land for it?"

"Is an unpardonable sinner before God."

"If he's killed?"

"The killer will inherit the eight heavens and not one less."

"There's someone here called Mahmood. He had donated land for the school." The Revered One ran his fingers through his hairy chest in anticipation. Mudalali's hands stroked his own ample belly.

"You have to cast a magic spell and make him mad."

"Umm."

"A plate with spells inscribed should be buried in that plot so that the building will collapse even if it were to come up."

"Umm."

"Don't worry about the expense it will involve."

"I'll first need to prepare some magic ink and observe."

"Do."

"We'll see. We could make him go mad."

"He has blackened my face before the village."

"Now we'll make him rub black on his own face."

Mudalali's countenance was now rid of the thunder clouds that had hovered over it. He relaxed in his seat, his composure restored.

The Revered One now sat cross-legged on the bed, put a pillow on the lap and dug his elbow into it.

"I'll have to perform many calculations after observing the ink solution. Will need to tend four or five fire-pits. At least six months will be needed to complete this."

"That's alright."

"But I have to go home."

"Has the jinn been recaptured?"

"I'll be imprisoning it in a day or two. It inhabits a rock that is in the middle of the sea. I've spotted it in the ink solution. Once it is captured, I leave."

"And after you leave?"

"I doubt if I shall return."

"I shall have none of it. You have to oblige me."

"As I said, it will take six months, not less."

"Let it be so."

"Won't my wife and children miss me?"

"We could send them money."

"That will hardly do. I am a husband and a father. Who'll send them love?"

"True enough."

"It won't be a bad idea if I marry here. I shall spend six more months here and hand over a neat job to Mudalali."

"This will be your. . . ."

"Fifth marriage."

Mudalali thought it over silently. A mute procession of fathers crossed his mind, followed by their young daughters—fair ones, dark ones, charming ones and some not-so-charming. Mudalali scratched his head and stroked his chin.

"We'll find a way."

"I wouldn't mind even if she is a widow."

"Let's see."

"Doesn't matter even if she is above thirty-five."

"Right."

"She might even be mother of a child or two."

"Right."

"She should be of the family type."

"Right."

Mudalali left the room and began pacing the verandah. It was dusk and lamps were being lit. Mudalali's shadow shook unsteadily in the moving flame.

Fragrant smoke curled from the joss sticks placed here and there. It was a Friday.

From the far corner of the house wafted the sweet notes of the Mohiuddin Prayer. Noohu Pattuma was singing, her voice brimming with sweetness and devotion. It cast a hold on Mudalali, forcing him to think deeply. The notes of the tune seemed strung in a fine thread of sorrow that was embedded in the heart's depth. Mudalali lowered his head. He stepped into the Mirror Hall and settled down in his favourite chair.

"Ayesha."

"Yes." Ayesha came running.

"Tell your Mami to sing softly."

That night Mudalali went to bed early. Doesn't matter even if she is a widow or is already mother of one or two children—the Revered One's words. What did he mean by what? Mudalali's thoughts got into a tangle that he couldn't unravel. It ruined his sleep. As a cock crowed in the wee hours of the morning, the eyes felt the strain of the burdensome night and a succession of bad dreams played themselves out. As the sky became lighter he opened his eyes and the first person they fell on was Avukkar.

"Avukkar, a marriage has to be arranged for the Revered One."

"What is the count?"

"Fifth."

"And if he were to go away soon?"

"It is permissible for a Revered One to marry wherever he happens to sojourn."

"On an earlier occasion also a Revered One married one of our women. Three children were born. Then he abandoned them. He sent them no money either. The family is poverty stricken even today."

"Revered Ones may marry anywhere they visit. Listen to me. Arrange a marriage."

"Why should I be singled out for this sin?"

"Because it is Ahamadu Kannu Mudalali of Northern House who so decrees."

"Since it is Mudalali's salt that I eat, I refuse to commit a sin for him."

15

Sema Kannu's fatiha ceremony was held with due pomp in the new house. Seven Lebbais took part in the Moulood recitation. The entire village was treated to a midday feast.

Hasanar Lebbai's school was invariably closed when such events took place. All his pupils would be found in front of the concerned house, awaiting a sumptuous meal. They would indulge in slanging matches, keep themselves busy with fistcuffs, the "China" hit, boxing and horseplay.

Hasanar Lebbai came out of Sema Kannu Mudalali's house letting out a contented belch. With some efforts, he dug out a tiny bit of meat that had lodged between his teeth and wiped his fingers against the wall.

Usan Pillai had closed the shop just to attend the fatiha feast. He had to wait outside the house for his turn and squatted in a corner, leaning against the wall. Moustache Mammaseen stood at the gate and pushed back the crowd with outstretched hands whenever they tried to barge into the house. Usan Pillai, a picture of patience, was impervious to the jostling crowd. Lebbai saw him drawing designs on the sand with a palm-rib.

"Haven't you eaten?"

"No."

"Who's in the shop?"

"I've closed it for the moment. How's the food?"

"Excellent. And as many helpings as one wants."

"Who's serving the meat?"

"Vappur Kannu. Serves generous chunks."

"Large-hearted, he is. Without a doubt. And I'll say it a second time."

"Let me have a puff of your beedi."

"I have only one—for my after-lunch puff."

"Give, I say. I'll have exactly two pulls at it and you can use it again."

Usan Pillai handed him a matchbox kept within a twist of his waist cloth.

"Beedi?"

"Inside the matchbox."

Lebbai opened the matchbox and found a half-burned stub. "Is this it?"

"That's all I have."

Lebbai lit the half-beedi and walked away. He was immediately stopped by Usan Pillai.

"Lebbai. Give it back so that I get at least one puff."

"But all it has is just one puff!"

"Never mind that."

Lebbai took a strong pull at the beedi and let out smoke through his nostrils. He handed it back to Usan Pillai who duly stubbed it and replaced it safely in the matchbox which in turn was tucked away in the waist cloth.

Hasanar Lebbai walked towards the rivulet that flowed by the cremation ground. A cool breeze was blowing. Lebbai removed his cap and cut across the coconut grove, heading north. Crossing the bridge he reached the main road from where he could observe the construction site of the Englees school. The foundation had been completed.

"Enemy. Come here to make infidels of us." He nodded to himself as though he had reached a decision.

He suddenly remembered that Mahmood had been sent for by Mudalali to appear before the Friday congregation. He spat out with vehemence in the direction of the school.

He retraced his steps along the river. The coconut fronds swayed gently, the cool clear water mirroring their reflection. The breeze had an inviting smell and Lebbai succumbed to it. He leaned against a tree and his eyes closed shut, a riot of pictures playing before him. Mahmood was tied to a pillar in the mosque all set to receive twenty-one blows with a bamboo stick that was wielded by Vappu. Mahmood squirmed in pain as the knotted rope held him back.

Lebbai laughed aloud.

Fisherwomen walking across the grove called out, "Erabbe. Laughing all by yourself?"

"Hmm. You stink terribly . . . go, go your way." He spat out in their direction. As soon as they were out of sight he recalled their blouseless appearance, their saris making up for the missing garment and their carefree gait. "Wives of the Devil." Lebbai got up and walked towards Mahmood's house. He knocked.

"Who is it?"

"It's me. Modin."

The door was opened by Mahmood's wife.

"Where's Mahmood?"

"Gone to the sea-shore."

"Tell him that he should present himself before Northern House Mudalali at the Friday congregation."

"What for?"

"I am conveying to you exactly what I was told to by Mudalali."

"I shall, when he is back."

It was late when Mahmood returned home. Pattakannu kept awake and opened the door after hearing the familiar three raps.

Her husband stood before her, body swathed in sweat, two shark fins in hand. A tired face confronted her, utterly alone in a night that spelled fear. It seemed to her that her husband's frail body contained within it God's very Creation.

"Give it fast, if you have something to eat."

"I made no kanji for the night," Pattumuttu said after a brief silence.

Mahmood listened in silence and gave the fins to his wife. Washing his limbs at the well, he settled down on a string cot.

"Is our daughter asleep?"
"Yes."
"I've found a groom for her."
"Where?"
"At Kulachhal. The boy isn't bad. Has a petty shop. Won't demand a big dowry."
"Is he good-looking?"
"Yes. The father is a fishmonger."
"My daughter for the son of a fishermonger?"
"Mind your tongue. Do we hail directly from Mecca? Our hearth wasn't even lit today. At least they have work to do everyday and the hearth is regularly lit. Isn't that enough, for family status? His father doesn't want more than ten sovereigns of gold on the daughter."
"What of the grove?"
"Didn't demand it. Still we should give it to our child."
"Have we anything more to give for expenses?"
"No."
"Have you finalized it?"
"No. I have requested for time." Mahmood lit himself a beedi.
"Modin had been here."
"That wretch? What for?"
"Mudalali wants you at the Friday congregation."
"He won't let me live in peace. Wants to harrass me for no reason at all."
"Did you say anything to provoke him?"
"I've said nothing offensive to Mr Big-Belly. He has gone crazy ever since I gave my land for the school. He's been telling everyone that I've turned an infidel. He's ordered Lebbai and the barber not to enter our doorstep."
"Why such extreme steps?"
"He's crazed in the extreme, that's why. He would like to see me tied to a pillar and beaten at the Friday congregation. Hence the summons."

"Rabbe," Pattakannu wailed.

"Even if so much as a speck of dust were to touch my body, the Northern House will be reduced to ashes. His canopied cart will roll over in the dust."

"We are poor and with a young daughter. It's we who should forbear."

"We are poor only in wealth. In strength of mind we are rich. My head will never bend before him. Never." Mahmood grit his teeth and thrust out a clenched fist which hit a nearby pillar. His hand hurt. Their daughter Suhra woke up in the commotion and found the father in a rage, eyes bloodshot.

"He knows that I have a young daughter in the house. That none will give his son to the daughter of a man who was delivered blows before a Friday congregation. So? Does he imagine that I'll fall at his feet? Never shall I do that. And I shall marry my daughter off. Without the barber, the village, the khateeb and Lebbai."

"How?"

"That's what Islam is about. Islam has never ruled that the Lebbai must perform a marriage. I can conduct my daughter's marriage if I know how to."

"What about registering in the mosque?"

"That register has no role in the Last Reckoning before God. He is not going to ask for it when we gather in the assembly for His Final Judgment." Mahmood sat quietly for a while, his hands supporting his bent head. All of a sudden he sprang to his feet and opened the door. The frontyard was wholly dark. The billowing clouds had swallowed the stars. From a distance came the hum of cicadas. A fox wailed from the rocky shore of the dilapidated Sheikh's Mosque. The strong winds carried a chill. The waves screamed incessantly and the breaking wavelets appeared to let out sobs.

"Ei! Light up some dry fronds."

"Where are you off to at the midnight hour?"

"I shall be back."

"Don't go."

"And who are you to order me?"
"Your wife."
"I must go now and ask him why he wants me."
"Don't." Pattakannu obstructed him at the door. Mahmood tugged at her hair to pull her out of his way.
"Vappa." Suhra sobbed loudly. Mahmood's grip loosened from his wife's hair. "Vappa, don't go."
"Your tears weaken my very bones." Mahmood sat down. The volcano stopped spewing and the lava remained within. The little mud lamp filckering all the while in a state of indecisiveness finally went out. The house sank into a darkness befitting the seventh sea.

16

Friday. The well at the mosque was crowded with people bathing and washing. The acrid smell of "Kama" brand blue soap pervaded the air. Little hillocks of froth surrounded the washing stone. Jabbar the barber, seated under a young coconut palm had started business before the sun's rays touched the ground. At eleven he was still busy and could find no way of relaxing his tired shanks. He hadn't managed to light even one beedi or empty his bladder. Customers waited impatiently for a shave or to shape a new beard or to have a tonsure.

Usan Pillai made sure that Mudalali's summons to Mahmood had reached every ear. He called anyone anyone and everyone who crossed the shop, all the while keeping himself busy rolling out beedis.

"Who's going there now?"

"It's me."

"Do come here. Are you aware why Mudalali has ordered Mahmood to come on Friday?"

"I wouldn't know."

"I see. So you'll be at the mosque on Friday, I hope?" Thus arrived the much-awaited Friday. Indeed a few had even put money into the donation box of the River-side mosque for the early arrival of that day. With sharpened ears they awaited the beats of the nagara drum that alerted them for the sermon.

Children crowded outside the mosque indulging in fights and fistcuffs accompanied by vocabulary that wouldn't spare even fathers and mothers.

Even before the nagara beats began to sound, men trickled in one by one into the mosque. The water in the tank moved incessantly like quickening heartbeats. The ladle and the coconut shell underwent repeated immersions. Specks of phlegm bordered the drain like unclaimed bodies.

The four halls of the mosque were full. Soon the beats of the nagara were sounded and Lebbai's call to the faithful floated in the air. The khateeb arrived and seated himself.

The gathering awaited the sound of Mudalali's footsteps with bated breath. The khateeb turned the pages of the book from which he intended to read the sermon. Every now and then his eyes peered into the distance.

Mahmood walked in, quick as lightening, and performed the ablutions. He was conscious of a thousand eyes boring into him. He entered the mosque and quietly sat down, leaning against a pillar. The clock's two hands moved like a signal. The khateeb looked at it and then towards Lebbai who in turn got up to proceed to Mudalali's house. Right at that moment Mudalali stepped in with Vappu in tow. His upturned moustache instilled fear in the crowd. They looked at Mahmood with trepidation, whose face betrayed no fear. He busied himself silently reciting to himself God's praises, his fingers keeping an automatic count.

The sermon was followed by the namaz and then the blessings, the du'a, and everyone sought God's grace with cupped palms. Soon they pushed and shoved one another for a place in the adjacent hall where Mudalali sat on the black stone. Next to him sat Syedna Mohammadu Mustafa Imbichi Koya, the Revered One.

Mahmood was the last man to leave the prayer congregation. He made his way through the throng to the exit with a nonchalance that left the crowd wonderstruck.

"Has he gone?" Mudalali enquired.

"Yes."

"Call him."

Hassanar Lebbai ran after Mahmood. "Mudalali wants you."

"What for?"

"I don't know."

"I cannot see him now." The voice was a roar. Without a second glance he walked out, ramrod straight.

"Hell will be let loose on him. He is no true Muslim who does not respect Mudalali," the whispering crowd ordained and looked expectantly at Mudalali.

"Vappu. Go and get him here."

"Hey you, stop."

"You mind your business."

"Mudalali calls you."

"Fetch him his wife."

"Talk properly, will you?"

"What if I won't?"

"I'll bash you up."

"Try and do it, you hairless one." Mahmood stopped and ran his fingers along the knife stuck into his waist belt. "I'll garland you with your own innards. Save your honour and get lost."

Vappu stiffened in his tracks. Mahmood walked away.

"Why didn't you get him?"

"He had a knife."

"A knife?"

"Yes."

"Subhanallah."

The gathering dispersed, one by one, let down by the turn of events. Mudalali and the Revered One were left to themselves. And Mahmood had walked away with such insolence!

★★★

Ahamadukannu Mudalali couldn't bring himself to eat even a handful of the rice that had been served before him. He got up suddenly, washed his hand and lowered himself into his favourite chair. The cheroot let out curls of black smoke.

Such a grave insult. He had been challenged openly before a Friday congregation! He felt a physical rot besetting him—the skin felt loose and his tongue seemed ready to drop off like a rotten banana.

The Western House fellows would naturally mock at him and do so again and again. That was inevitable. The flagpole which flaunted the proud banner of his unchallenged status now had a dent. A dent that couldn't be straightened. Caused not even by a man of means, worth at least a mention and fit enough to fight a battle with, but by an ordinary villager who lived to the east of the memorial rock. Whose sin was it that he suffered such lose of face? His forefathers' or his own? Or was this the first phase of his destruction?

Mudalali did not stir from the chair even when the call for the evening prayers was sounded. The black tea that had been kept near the chair had turned cold and remained untouched despite reminders from Farid. All that Mudalali saw before him was the mosque, the throng, the black stone-seat. And Vappu with his upturned moustache.

Around nine in the night Mudalali got up from his chair and called out to a sleepy Avukkar.

"Start right away."

"Where to?"

"To Tiruvitankotu."

"Can't it wait till light?"

"No."

"It's too dark."

"No, you've to go right away. And be there by dawn. Let the cart be readied at once."

"But. . . ."

"No more ifs and buts. Agree to all their demands. Finalize the marriage."

"Alright."

"We'll be giving the girl gold ornaments worth a hundred sovereigns and five acres of coconut plantations. And plenty by way of pomp and show."

"What if they want to see the girl?"

"They may come here."

"Okay."

"And not a word should reach them about the day's happenings at the mosque. It is a matter of great shame for us. The marriage must take place before the news leaks out. Within this month."

"Okay."

"Get going."

Avukkar got into the swift-moving personal bullockcart of Mudalali and the two white bullocks trotted ahead, their neck bells tinkling. The little lantern tied in the axle threw forth the wheels' shadow as they kept turning.

Farid overheard everything that his uncle had told Avukkar. He could picture before him a bejewelled Ayesha, swathed in costly silks and a gold-laced upper-cloth covering her head, getting into the carriage. It was as though a snake had bitten him. He searched for her like one demented and at last found her in her room, sobbing silently. He gazed at her, tethering his surging emotions with great difficulty.

"Ayesha. Avukkar has just left to finalize your marriage." He walked away the very instant, neither seeing nor hearing her.

17

The fiery heat of a noon sun was slowly yielding up its strength. The breeze, that had turned and rolled all the while in the fury of the heat, began to cool from within. The gathering squatting on the front bench of Asan's chukku neer shop got busy, keening on a bullock cart that rolled down swiftly from the north.

The cart stopped at the shop. A young man dressed in modern trousers got down. The assembly on the front bench quickly and silently made for the shop's interior. Asan, busy doling out the ginger-molasses concoction watched through the small window. His customers, busy quaffing the liquid with bites of tapioca wafers, craned their necks and looked. "He is a white man," observed one of them.

"No, it's just his complexion."

"What do you make of his dress, then?"

"White men have cat-eyes. This one's eyes are black."

"Then he must be one of our countrymen."

"Can you tell me where the new school is?"

"Chool?"

"Yes, school."

"What exactly is a chool?"

"A reading place."

"Oh that. You can see it from further down, this direction."

"Thanks." The stranger left.

Asan enquired: "What exactly did he mutter when he left?"

"That's what isn't clear to me either. Perhaps he hurled a bad word at us."

"It didn't sound like a bad word."

"Who's he?"

"Perhaps a government man who has come to see the new reading place."

The cart trundled ahead, leaving a cloud of dust in its wake. Two men followed it in idle curiosity. Hasanar Lebbai approaching them from the opposite direction stood on one side to let the cart pass. He widened his eyes questioningly at the two men who answered him, gesturing with their hands, in the negative.

Lebbai now went to observe the cart from the vantage point of the bridge. The cart had stopped near the new school. "Let's see who it is."

The young man got down. He had a curly head of hair. Lebbai studied him, head to toe, from the distance. The young man put him off.

The young man observed the curious men who had gathered around him with a friendly smile.

"So you all belong to this place?"

"Yes."

"Are there many houses here?"

"Yes."

"Belonging to all communities, I suppose?"

"Yes. But Muslims are more."

"Is there a school in the neighbouring village?"

"Luckily, there exists no such thing in these parts."

"It's a good thing then for you to start a school here."

"A good thing? Says who? It's going to ruin us."

"Ruin you?"

"What else? We fellows have never sinned nor swayed from our fasts and prayers. Now this Iblis school sprouts up here just to destroy our faith. And it's all the fault of that blackguard Mahmood."

"Will faith be destroyed if you study?"

"What else? We'll die infidels. And let's not forget, we have an account to give on the Day of Reckoning."

"But haven't many of us studied?"

"You're all a crowd of infidels. We are Muslims—followers of the Fourth and Final Book. Know that."

"I too am a Muslim."

"What?" The Lebbai was surprised. For the first time in his life he saw a Muslim wearing trousers, with cropped hair too. It was simply not credible.

Hasanar Lebbai gave the young man a steady once-over. Time and its turns, he told himself.

"What do you call yourself?"

"Mehboob Khan."

"'Kan' what?"

"Mehboob Khan."

"So the name too is Englees."

"No, it's not an English name."

"It is Englees. Mamma Kannu, Nooh Kannu, Aimakannu—these are Muslim names, pure Arabic names. For the first time, I hear today a name that won't blend with our speech. 'Kan' and 'Keen.' Whoever heard of such names? Here we know only one 'Can'—and that's kept in the mosque."

"I don't understand."

"There is a can there into which we urinate."

He laughed. A good crowd had collected by now which looked at Lebbai with blatant admiration and wonder.

Hasanar Lebbai now moved closer and aimed a question at the visitor, his tone mock-conspiratory.

"You said you are a Muslim. How then do you wear this nonsensical garment and manage to urinate? And wash yourself?"

A question worth asking—the crowd nodded in assent. Hasanar Lebbai was visibly pleased. His chest swelled. The ribcage touched the half-sleeved collar-less shirt with its blood stains left behind by crushed bed bugs.

Mehboob Khan was in a dilemma and at a loss to answer so crudely-put a question. Everyone stared into his face in anticipation as he thought, "Can one answer such men? They have neither knowledge nor culture, not even to a minute degree. Their religious faith has degenerated into a blind adherence from which they may never surface. And here I am, to teach their offspring. I should not be surprised if I am occasionally left alone in an empty classroom."

"What's this? You're hardly talking?"

It was Lebbai. Mehboob Khan broke the chain of thought and once more took in the surroundings. The line that curved before him presented a row of men with tonsured heads and round topis. Their waist-cloths fell just below their knees and on their shoulders lay a second piece of cloth. Rustic men they were.

"Come on, tell us. So, do you stand and urinate?"

"No."

"Don't tell lies."

"I sit on my haunches."

"How can you bend the knees?"

"I can."

"Then demonstrate, here and now."

"I don't need to, not now."

"We aren't fools. You needn't dupe us."

"I am not here to cheat you. I am here to teach your children their abc's, I am to teach in this school."

"The followers of the Third Book are infidels. And they send an Englees Muslim here to make us infidels," a voice burst out. Hasanar Lebbai raised his arms as if to calm down the outburst.

"Patience, patience." He now turned to Mehboob Khan. "Look, can you deny that you're here to make us infidels? Your name is an Englees name. Your clothes are Englees. You have an infidel's head. Alright, let that be. But to teach, you aren't going to get our children. And never will you enter our mosque, claiming that you're a Muslim. I hope I am clear to you," Hasanar Lebbai said his piece in a loud voice and left. For the faithful had to be called for the evening prayers.

Mahboob Khan took out his belongings from the cart, which moved away immediately. As he watched the wheels turnings in the dust he fought strongly an urge to go back in it. Why not confess that he didn't want a teacher's job in the village?

No, that couldn't be. Who but he would want to change this benighted society? Which outsider would want to do it? He had to ensure that there was a dawn here. People had to be forced to open their eyes and made to come out of the bog of superstition that had consigned them to an abyss. Troubles he was certainly going to have to face, yes. But surely one should bear that much for the sake of one's community.

A cup of tea was all that he'd had towards evening. No dinner could be got anywhere around. The sole hotel in the village was Asan's chukku neer shop. A fresh problem confronted him—where to find food?

It was a five-mile walk to a hotel on a rough road, full of peaks and troughs, that had never been visited by an autobus.

Hunger gnawed at his stomach. He stretched himself on a bench, supporting his head on his forearm. He lay in utter darkness, eyes wide awake. The continuous pangs of hunger felt like the moving legs of crab on the sides of his stomach and warded off sleep. Even a matchbox couldn't be found that he might at least take a look at the watch.

At midnight, as a cool breeze blew in from the sea, his eyes closed in fatigue.

The silence was suddenly shattered when a heavy object was hurled at the entrance.

Mehboob Khan held his breath. Not a sound escaped his frightened being.

Again the same noise. It was obvious that someone wanted to scare him. Mehboob Khan groped about in the dark and at last succeeded in opening the door.

He could faintly discern two figures running away.

Mehboob Khan kept a lone vigil through the rest of the night.

18

The sea had yielded a rich haul. The shore resounded with the cacophony of the fisherfolk.

The air was laden with the smell of fish. Kites circled the sky. Crows sat on the palms looking for an opportune moment to steal fish. Children roamed in hordes with small boxes to put little fish into. The village beggars were out in strength.

Mahmood walked to where the fish hauls were auctioned, with a rolled up gunny bag stuck between body and forearm. He felt a rough-textured nudge against his elbow. Mahmood turned, to find Usan Pillai with a palm-strip fish basket.

Usan Pillai called Mahmood to his side, winking. He then whispered into his ears.

"Want to know the latest?"

"No."

"There's utter confusion."

"What about?"

"Our village is soon to be afflicted by pestilence."

"What d'you mean?"

"The Revered One has let loose the jinn."

"Revered One who?"

"The Revered One who was a guest in the Northern House. He quarreled with Mudalali and left."

"What did they quarrel about?"

"A pity that I've to say this. The Revered One pecked not only from the plate before him but from the winnowing tray as well. He wanted to marry Mudalali's sister and the two exchanged words. The Revered One is a proud man after all. He got angry and walked out during the night."

"So the evil has left at last?"

"You shouldn't speak like this. Remember, he is a Revered One from the Islands. Even if you speak from the other shore of the sea he can hear it on this shore. Such are his powers."

"Mudalali is a fodder-filching stray and he entertains anyone declaring himself to be a holy man. He deserves everything that happened."

"Don't let it out that I told you. It was Hasanar Lebbai who put it into my ears."

Usan Pillai walked eastward. Mahmood saw the sea. Catamarans and boats tore through the waves that glistened white in the sun.

Is the mind too a sea? So full was it with memories moving forever, wave upon wave.

If the womenfolk of the Northern House were insulted, was it not like a slur on the womenfolk of his own house? A woman is a woman, to whichever house she may belong. A woman should be respected.

When efforts were on to find a suitable girl for the Revered One's fifth marriage, Mahmood had opposed and with strong reason. He would marry and live with the woman for a month or two, and walk out. That was a sin, never to be acquiesced to. Perhaps, he hadn't been too keen on those matches. He must have set his eyes on Noohu Pattuma. And that must have led him to declare his intent for a fifth marriage. Whatever it might have been, the village was well rid of him, thanks perhaps to someone's good deeds.

Mahmood's forehead was covered with sweat. He treated himself to a cup of buttermilk from the vending woman to smooth his dry throat. Letting out a belch, he walked towards the west.

★ ★ ★

Ahamadu Kannu Mudalali came to know of the arrival of the teacher of the Englees School. That he was a Muslim. That he wore trousers like the white man who followed the Third Book. His blood boiled and his eyes glinted with rage. His jaws tightened.

"Use a thorn to remove a thorn."

"Yes," agreed Avukkar. "The English teacher is here to see Mudalali."

"I shall never gaze into the face of man who has cropped his hair."

"That's the day's fashion."

"He's an infidel. There's no need to see him. Tell him to leave."

"I've already said that. He has come to request that Mudalali tell the children of the village to attend his school."

"He isn't going to get any Muslim child as his student."

"There's already one Muslim student."

"And who's the bastard's father?"

"He's Mahmood's son."

Mudalali stood still as if in a shock. He then broke his own silence. "Don't count him into the community. The entire village has boycotted him. He is an infidel and so is his son."

"I shall then tell him that he won't get any Muslim boy for the school."

Avukkar was about to leave.

"Wait, is he sitting or standing?"

"Sitting."

"Where?"

"On the bench."

"Make sure that you wash it with seven buckets of water and recite the kalma over it."

Avukkar left. Mudalali walked towards the room occupied by the Revered One. The door was open. Mudalali went in and sat down on a chair opposite the Revered One. The two studied each other silently for a few minutes.

"You haven't pulled off what you had promised," Mudalali began. "The school building has come up and studies have begun."

"I am quite aware."

"Then what happens to my request?"

"I told that day itself that I am a husband. It's been three months since I came here."

"I did bring forth a couple of proposals but you showed no interest."

"Why should I have marry women I don't like? I hail from the Islands. My father Muttukoya had disciples by the thousands. My grandfather Syed Alavikoya was a great seer. I am his grandson. How can I marry into common folk?"

"Do indicate your preference. I did see a couple of possible matches that you might have liked. But that wretch Mahmood meddled and upset my plans."

"Forget what didn't happen and think of what can happen."

"Yes, why not?"

"That depends upon the kindness of your great self. Let the marriage take place; the very next day I promise to deliver the ruins of the school. I shall reveal before you the sight of a fleeing teacher. I shall ensure a Mahmood with maimed limbs. All I shall need is a fire-pit."

"How could the Revered One presume that I'd be anything but generous towards his great self? God knows how much I have endured."

"I won't beat about the bush. I'll come straight to the point."

"Do tell me."

"You should raise no objection."

"Do I dare?"

"Good."

Ahamadukannu Mudalali looked into the Revered One's face. The Revered One turned and shut the open windows in the rear. He sat on the bed and put a pillow on his lap, resting his elbows on it. He ran his fingers through his beard.

"Mudalali's sister Noohu Pattuma should be wedded to me."

A strange sound escaped from the mouth of Ahamadu Kannu Mudalali. His eyes riveted on the person of the Revered One. As a darkness surrounded him, he discerned the sharp claws of a tiger's paws poised to spring.

"Why don't you talk?" The Revered One asked Mudalali, with a forced smile on his lips. He was closely observing Mudalali, to see if his lips moved. They didn't. He tapped him gently on the thigh with a reed pen used for writing the incantations on China plates. "Why don't you say something?"

Mudalali opened his eyes as if waking from sleep and confronted a smiling Revered One. The smile seemed to him a swaying hooded snake. It's sharp poisonous fangs seemed to be lodging themselves deep all over his body. The poison was spreading slowly. From the toes up through the veins, through marrow and muscle, now reaching the heart. The head felt swollen, ready to burst into pieces. It might burst right now, he thought.

"Mudalali."

Mudalali blinked his eyes and looked at the Revered One.

"Did you hear what I said?"

"Yes."

"So you agree?"

"I am tired."

"You may think it over."

Mudalali got up. He steadied himself putting his hand against the wall, slowly he propelled himself to his favourite chair and leaned back.

He had not for a moment thought that the Revered One would have such thoughts. Yes, he did feel once or twice that the Revered One was throwing hints in that direction but he hadn't paid any heed. He had thought that he was probably reading wrong meanings into them. Now, it was out. The Revered one had now made himself clear beyond doubt.

Surely it did not behove a guest to train his thoughts on such a goal.

Under no circumstance would Noohu Pattuma be given in marriage to him. He had proclaimed himself a Revered One and he was believed. Was he actually worthy? Who could tell? Should a woman of a well-known family such as theirs, of such proud lineage, be given away in marriage to a man whose name, village and address were unknown? A woman who was the daughter of Shakhul Hameedu Pillai of the Northern House? No, this won't happen. Not in the Northern House.

Will she agree? No. She would never. She had had to remove her taali in her fourteenth year and put on white clothes. Not a single strand of coloured thread had touched her body hence nor as much as a speck of gold.

A number of proposals came for her and he had dutifully conveyed them to her. But she declined them with a finality. "I've removed one taali. I don't ever want to wear a second one around my neck." Ahamadu Kannu had had to give up. And now, her youth withering away after it had dutifully bloomed as ordained by time, would she consent to a marriage? No, never.

Mudalali smoked cheroot after cheroot. Its blood red eye emitted smoke as its top was strangulated between tense fingers. The Mirror Hall was full of the acrid smoke of burnt tobacco.

The Revered One may leave him in a fit of anger. That would be dangerous. He might practice black magic or let loose an evil spirit on him.

The school now stood solid and square, mocking him. Mahmood had thrown an open challenge at him and carried on, without a befitting answer from him. Would the rest of his life be spent carrying this burden of defeat? Would the school bell always chime to echo against the walls of his mind? Would Mahmood continue to walk, treading his very head? It was as though he was hung with hooks from his collars, disabled from moving to the right or to the left. Like a defenceless woman held from either side by two toughs, with nowhere to escape. His thoughts were like maimed feet groping weakly for escape routes. He called out aloud to Avukkar.

Avukkar, busy washing the bench and chanting the kalma over it, ran to his master, hands still wet.

"It's all darkness before me. Show me the way," Mudalali shut his eyes.

Avukkar stood before his master, a picture of humility, not understanding a word. He observed the Mudalali closely. The face was pale and his lips dry. Cheroot ends littered the floor.

"Avukkar Pillai, find me a means."

"What should I do?"

"I never imagined this of the Revered One."

"What's the matter?"

"The Revered One wants to wed Nuvattuma."

"What?" Avukkar was shocked. "Wants to marry the daughter of Shakhul Hameedu Pillai of the Northern House? No, it's not right."

"That's what I thought too. Is he indulging in black magic?"

"Possibly."

"Might even let loose an evil spirit."

Avukkar had no words this time.

"Is he likely to place her under his spell and drag her with him?"

"He is capable of that."

"I've a doubt. Could he have changed her mind?"

"He could do that too."

"We'll talk to her and find out what she thinks."

"If Sister agrees, is the marriage to take place?"

"Isn't that better than to have to face her elopement? If he casts a spell on her and entices her can we stick to our lives?"

"True enough."

"Alright. You may go now."

Mudalali got up from the elephant leg chair. Tightening the waist-cloth, he put on his slippers. With resounding steps he walked into the second courtyard, moving the curtain aside. Farid was sitting on his haunches on top of the wooden chest, his body looking shrunk. The face was devoid of its usual cheer.

"What's ailing you?"

"It's nothing." He went out.

"Viyattuma," Mudalali called his wife.

"Coming." The voice came from near the well, where she was busy in pre-prayer ablutions.

"Where is Nuvattuma?"

"She's here."

"Tell her to come here."

Mudalali sat on top of the chest. Nuvattuma came and stood in front her Kaka.

"Did you call me?"

"I did. I have to ask you something."

Noohu Pattuma cracked her knuckles nervously, wondering what it might be about. What did Kaka want? Ayesha's marriage was going to be conducted with borrowed money. The coconut merchant had already refused a loan. Three plantations had already been sold quietly to an outsider. Perhaps he needed her thumb impression to sell one of hers? Or perhaps her jewels were to be pledged to raise money?

"I want to ask you something. You should be frank. You needn't feel shy to express yourself. If you desire it, it will take place. Otherwise we'll forget about it."

"Kaka should be free to tell me whatever he wants."

"In this matter, it's your opinion that will be final. You are the mother of a grown-up son. You must decide."

"Do tell, Kaka."

"You know the Revered One who's staying with us?"

"Yes."

"Are you willing to marry him?"

She turned her face away sharply. "I am interested in marriage with nobody. Once is enough. If Kaka finds me and my son burdensome, the two of us can jump into a river or well." Noohu Pattuma sobbed. "How did Kaka have the heart to tell me this? So the widowed sister and her idiot son are a burden on Kaka. We'll both give up our souls."

"Allah! Please don't think all this. I just asked, that's all. Do collect yourself. And don't discuss this with anyone." Mudalali stood a while, hanging his head.

He walked straight into his guest's room. He stared hard into the face of the Revered One. Eager expectation was writ large upon it. Let him do black magic or let loose a spirit. There were bigger men who could control his power. Expense was hardly a consideration in such matters.

"Please sit down."

"No."

"Why is your face rather different."

"It's nothing. You had wished to marry my sister, isn't it?"

"Yes."

"That cannot happen."

"That cannot happen?" The expression on his face changed.

"Most certainly it cannot."

The Revered One got up from the cot. "I've nothing more to do with this place. I shall leave this very moment."

"You may leave whenever it suits you." The Revered One's keen ears heard Mudalali's footsteps sounding more and more distant.

19

It was ten o'clock. The school bell hanging like a dead body in a noose in the front yard suddenly came to life.

Shirtless children busy playing in the sand in the open courtyard now rushed back into the classroom and occupied the few benches that lay there. The din was however kept on.

The teacher entered the classroom. "Salaam Sar." The children jumped down from their perch and shouted in unison.

"Silence." The teacher rapped the stick that he had taken out from behind the black board. He took out the attendance book and called out the names:

"Appu Kuttan."
"Asar."
"Ganesan Achari."
"Kasar."
"Santa Kumaran Nayar."
"Hajar."
"Valliyamma."
"Ajar."
"Pir Mohammadu?"
"Asar."

Pir Muhammad had been dubbed baldie by his fellow-students. Pir Muhammad would retort: "Sons of pigs. Infidel dead-wood."

"Pir Mohammad. Stand up." The teacher ordered. Pir Mohammad stood up. He had tied his father's shoulder-cloth around his waist. It loosened and fell. Pir Mohammad shook like a leaf as the teacher quelled him with a severe look through white lenses. He forgot to pick up the cloth.

"Wear it."

Pir Mohammadu did as he was told.

"Will you talk again in the classroom?"

The boy shook his head. With an effort he dammed the drops that were about to fall from his eyes.

"Sit down."

"Pick up your slates and slate-pencils."

The children picked up the slates that lay on the mud floor that had been laved with cowdung.

"Wipe the slates."

The children spat on their respective slates and rubbed them with their fingers. The slates were wiped with whatever garment they wore.

"Put down the slates."

"Stand up."

"Sit down."

Everybody performed obediently.

"Now for some arithmetic. I'll pose the problem and you'll answer."

"Yes, Saar."

"What is five and five?"

The teacher observed the faces. "Narayanan?"

Narayanan stood up. He scratched the dirt on his out-curved belly and stared vacantly at the teacher.

"Next, Murugan?" Murugan couldn't answer either.

"Next. Pir Mohammad. What is five and five?"

Pir Mohammad thought it over. The answer burst forth happily, like a fire cracker. "A very big five, big as an elephant's head."

"Like your father's head. Sit down. Next. Valliyamma?"

Valliyamma stood up with a dumb face. None knew the answer.

The teacher was about to solve the problem on the blackboard when a stranger was seen outside the classroom. Without as much as a by-your-leave the stranger walked straight into the classroom.

"Come here, you. First go buy fish from the shore and then come back to read. It's too cheap to be missed." He dragged a boy away from the classroom.

The teacher was taken aback. He came up to the door and quietly watched the father and son march away. Were he to remonstrate he would be probably subjected to blows. They were illiterate to the core and as rough as they came. An earlier incident was still fresh in his mind. He had administered a rap on the thigh of a mulish student who refused to repeat the lesson after him despite his patient efforts. The student had wept.

When he came back from home after his midday meal his father accompanied him. The latter confronted the teacher. "Who exactly do you think you are to dare hit the son that I have sired?" The enraged father had asked. He had had no answer. "Come on. Enough of learning in this man's school, to the accompaniment of beatings."

The boy didn't come back to school.

A negligible number had enrolled in the school. And that number kept dwindling, day by day. At this rate, he would probably lose the job during the next inspection. The inspector had already warned him, the week after the school opened. There were only ten students. "This won't do. There should be at least thirty students."

He had met Mudalali that day and had been depressed at the turn of events. But give up he wouldn't. He knocked at every door in the village and talked about the his mission. All that merely exposed him to baleful glances that felt like poison-tipped darts. He had but to bear them and with patience. As he reached the school, he was about to break down. He remained in a depression unaware of the slipping hours. He was lulled to sleep by the cool breeze and the consolation of having enrolled one Muslim student.

He resolved to teach the children with patience and affection, completely eschewing harsh language and beatings. He entertained them with funny stories and indulged them with sweets. The enrollment went up to sixteen and just as quickly dropped down to eleven. On an average, three of them wouldn't be present daily. The teacher neither scolded nor punished his pupils.

The teacher was keenly observing the movements of the table clock. The children knew that the lunch time break was near.

As the bell was about to be rung they rushed out. "Salaam Sir."

Mahboob Khan locked the doors and gave the keys to the watchman. He was hungry, having had to go without breakfast that morning. It was some distance from school to home.

"Home" was an old unused shop without the benefit of a bathroom or latrine, for which he paid a rent of two rupees. It meant an early morning or late night trip into a grove to clear the bowels. Water had to be fetched from a well in the adjoining grove. Behind "home" was a make-shift shed covered with coconut fronds which was used as a urinal.

A daily diet of puttu and tapioca made palatable by powdered red chilli and dry coconut kernel had begun to tell on his intestines.

It was ages since Mahboob Khan had set his eyes on rice. He went home on a holiday and brought his wife to try to make a home of the old shop.

The following day Mahboob Khan's wife walked to the well with a pot poised against her hip. Instantly she became the object of the womenfolk's curiosity who took time off to stare at her. Cringing, she avoided their glances and reached the well, where a group of women faced her. As each pair of eyes bored through her body which had turned stiff and self-conscious. She clung to the pot and chewed her nails and was unable to look up.

Each of the women muttered something audibly and winked at one another. The younger ones suppressed their laughter conspicuously, placing their palms on their mouths. Some gazed at her in unabashed wonder. A few felt her fair skin. Her ears presented a strange sight with neither the traditional ornament nor the requisite holes.

"Woman, didn't your father and mother arrange to get your ears properly pierced?"

"No."

"What's your name like?'

"Noor Jehan."

"Where's this name from?"

"It's an Englees name," volunteered one.

"Have you borne children?"

"No."

Immediately a pair of eyes probed for any visible stretch marks around her navel.

"Who are you, girl?"

"Wife of the schoolmaster."

"Allah! We can't follow this. Speak our tongue. Are you the wife of the postoffice man?"

"No. The schoolmaster's wife?"

"She is the wife of that trouser-wearing Englees-man teacher."

"I see."

"Are you Muslim?"

"Yes."

"Why have you worn a sari around you like an infidel woman wanting to go to hell?"

There was no reply.

One woman nudged at another. Her eyes pointedly looked at the strap of the bodice that was visible underneath Noor Jehan's blouse.

"Look, you! A male's undergarment underneath her jumper."

"It's not a male's garment. It is a 'Vadi'." A second woman corrected the first.

"Are you totally without shame?"

Noor Jehans' eyes remained glued to the ground.

Suddenly a woman observed the petticoat border that peeped slightly beneath Noor Jehan's sari.

"Look, you, another wonder! A garment underneath her sari too!"

"Let's see." A woman bent down to lift the sari. Noor Jehan jerked her hand off and walked away.

"Look at her, the hip-swinging vadi-wearing woman."

Noor Jehan placed the empty pot before her husband. Her eyes were little pools. "Take me home. I cannot live in the midst of these women."

"Didn't they let you fetch water?"

"They ask me all kinds of repulsive questions. I will not go again to fetch water." She was now sobbing.

"Don't be upset. They must have been curious about your sari and jumper. They are rustic women, after all. I shall go and fetch the water."

Mahboob Khan picked up the pot and walked to the well. His unforeseen appearance put the women to flight. Mahboob Khan was about to plunge the bucket into the well. Suddenly a woman's voice rang out behind the hedge.

"Isn't this a woman's job? What is a man doing here? Send your wife, if you want water."

Mahboob Khan put down the bucket. Without a word he walked back, with an empty pot. None was there to share his sorrow, none to divide his burden.

As the lunch hour came to an end, Mahboob Khan's thoughts once again converged on the school, dispelling the recollections of the past hour.

20

"Daughter, all this is fate. A woman has to bear this and more. Learn patience, daughter. The Creator sees and hear all." Noohu Pattuma gently stroked her niece's curly hair and spoke words of consolation. The latter sat near the bedstead with bent head, not once looking at the aunt, despite all her entreaties. "Come and eat something. Don't keep on sitting on the same spot."

"I needn't."

"You can't get away like that. You can't fast this way."

"The consequences are mine alone."

"Don't talk nonsense. Eat and bathe and dress at the right hours. Don't shun people. Since you came back you've spoken to no one."

"My dearest aunty. Leave me to myself."

Noohu Pattuma gave up. She knew that her efforts would be of no use. Ayesha had always been a stubborn one. Adulthood had made no difference to that. As Noohu Pattuma came out she saw Farid sitting on the wooden store with a tired face. Ever since Ayesha's return home he had looked sad and cheerless. He barely spoke and a dullness weighed upon all his actions. Noohu Pattuma stood observing him but he didn't acknowledge her presence. He moved out of the passage. His head and chin had several day's growth on them. It had been days since he'd had a bath.

Why this sudden change? Noohu Pattuma was hard put to know. The change occured after Ayesha came back from her husband's. He was no more the cheerful and energetic lad that he was. Perhaps she had told him her story. But was he sharp enough to understand her?

"Why are you behaving like one mad?" She had asked him once.

"I am a mad man. I suffer from madness." The conversation over, he went out.

She must have said something to him. He might have understood it. The thought of it must be the reason behind his sadness.

"Ayeshamma, did you tell Farid anything about the son-in-law," she had asked Ayesha. Ayesha wouldn't open her mouth.

Silence reigned in the Northern House since Ayesha returned to her parental home. Fatigue was writ large on everyone's faces. Mudalali didn't utter more than a few words everyday. Ayesha's mother charged her husband each night with being responsible for the turn of events. Why did he marry off the daughter into a far-off house. Why did he not make proper enquires about the groom? Why did he bother himself only with his family status and wealth?

Mudalali lay curled up in the easy-chair and smoked non-stop. The burden of having no answers weighed heavily on his head.

"He's here." Avukkar presently announced in all humility.

"Who?"

"The registrar."

Mudalali sat upright. "Call the writer."

Govinda Pillai presented himself with a few documents. He tied his shoulder-cloth across his waist and greeted Mudalali with folded hands.

"How many, Govinda Pillai?"

"Three groves."

Mudalali got up from the chair and sat before the registrar.

"Do you hereby make a sale of three groves to Muttayyan Nadar, son of Kutti Nadar?"

"Yes."

"Have you received the payment?"

"Yes."

A liveried assistant rubbed Mudalali's left thumb on a board that had been coated with ink. He pressed his thumb on the official paper on which was printed a picture of Srimulam Tirunal Rama Varma Maharaja.

Plantations bearing the survey numbers 2693, 2320 and 2241 now belonged to Muttayya Nadar. This was the prelude for more such agreements that would come about in due course.

Mudalali came back and sat in his usual chair and lit a cheroot.

This was one of the many agreements made in order to borrow money for Ayesha's marriage to make it the grand affair that it was. Sixty goats had been slaughtered and the feast had lasted seven days. Indeed there had never been so grand an affair before. It was like a resounding slap on the face of the Western House Mudalali. Ayesha was covered in gold from head to toe. Even her anklets were made of gold. Her golden waist belt had bud-shaped ends of solid gold.

The daughter and son-in-law got into a coach covered with silk curtains. The mother hugged and kissed the daughter and wept. The aunt hugged her neice and shed tears. Penetrating her zari veil and a film of tears, Ayesha's eyes riveted themselves on Farid's face, who was standing at a distance. Tears were all that she could share with him. Farid's eyes were fixed on the wet streaks on Ayesha's cheeks which glistened through the veil. As he bit his lips to quieten his heart, she could hear its silent language.

As the horse pranced forward, with its gay crest fluttering and the neck-bell tinkling, Farid felt a part of his heart go dead. His eyes now freely poured out their grief. Even as his eyes thirsted for a glimpse of those glistening cheeks, the coach rolled out of sight. "Ayesha," he told himself. "Forget me. I am a mad man. But never shall I forget you. Not as long as my breath stays imprisoned in this throat."

But so much had changed within a month. Tears streaked her cheeks now too. The cheeks are red now as they were then. But how different the reasons.

Ayesha didn't spend even a full month in her husband's house. She had arrived alone one evening with her bridal box.

Everybody was puzzled. Her mother questioned her. Ayesha merely sobbed. Her father tried to talk to her. She wept, face covered. She lay on the cot totally dishevled and for three days didn't touch food. Mudalali called Avukkar.

"You have to go tommorrow."

"Where?"

"To Ayesha's in-laws."

"I shall."

"You've to find out why Ayesha is back."

"I shall." Avukkar left at dawn.

He was not back even at nine in the night. The village had shrunk back into the womb of darkness. Mudalali could hear the baying fox from the washerman's rock and the dogs barking. . . . But the sound of hooves defied his ears. The clock kept up its steady motion. From the south came the roar of the sea. Mudalali walked towards the Revered One's room in search of consolation, only to find it locked. He remembered that its occupant had left a few days ago.

Perhaps he should keen his ears to the breeze. Yes. There was the sound of bells and it was coming nearer and nearer. Mudalali got up and went to the main gate with a hurricane lamp. As Avukkar got down from the carriage, Mudalali held up the lamp. Avukkar's face was pale as death.

"What happened?"

"Come in. I shall tell."

Mudalali sat on the easy-chair. "Tell me."

"First, you must grant me forgiveness. For it is I who brought about this marriage."

"What happened?"

"It is this sinner who did it." Avukkar's throat was hoarse. Viyattuma stood behind the curtain to hear what Avukkar had to say. Avukkar stuttered it out, groping for expression.

"The new son-in-law is mad."

"Oh my God!" Mudalali slapped hard on his chest and collapsed into the chair falling on his side.

"Oh my Martyrs of Badr!" Viyattuma could be heard beating her chest.

21

"Who crops his hair?" Lebbai put the question before one of his students.

"An infidel."

"Good. So what is the man who teaches in the Englees school?"

"An infidel." The noise resounded. Lebbai rapped his stick on the floor. "Should one then study in a place where the teacher is an infidel?"

"No. It's a sin to do that. Allah will burn such persons in the fires of hell."

"Good boys. Will any of you ever go to read those crooked alphabets?"

"Never, Elebbe."

Lebbai laughed with pride revealing his betel-stained teeth. As he did so, a spray of saliva descended. A boy shouted, expertly disguising his voice: "Rain, wonderful rain."

"Which bastard is this?" There was pin-drop silence.

"The pimps. I shall beat you all and skin you alive." He rolled his eyes and glowered at the children. "You may go now. Be here early tomorrow."

The children ran out, the commotion like that of dammed waters being released. One of them chanted rhythmically: "Elebbe, elebbe, he."

"Who's that bastard?" Lebbai arrived on the scene rapping his stick. The children ran harder and disappeared out of sight.

He brought out his collar-less shirt that had been folded and rolled and kept behind the blackboard. He put on his grimy cap and wound around it a torn black-bordered all-purpose cloth. He cleaned the knife used for slitting the throat of fowls and stuck it into his belt.

He walked in the direction of Usan Pillai's shop. The latter peered at Lebbai through his lenses, which he adjusted, pushing them up.

"Give me one."

Usan Pillai concentrated on his beedi-rolling tray as though he had not beard Lebbai.

"I feel rather bad in the mouth. Give me a beedi for just one pull. I'll share a secret with you."

Usan Pillai obliged with alacrity at the mention of a "secret."

"Why can't you spare me a whole beedi?" Lebbai lit the beedi with the glowing tip of the rope-lighter.

"Don't throw the butt. Give it to me." Usan Pillai stretched out his fingers to take the beedi after Lebbai took a pull at it. Usan Pillai managed to get something yet out of the butt. His cheeks were drawn in, almost touching each other.

Lebbai coughed and spat out the phlegm. "I am no more the Lebbai you know."

"Then?"

"I am a new Lebbai." He settled down on the wooden plank in front of the shop.

"Usan Pillai, what's your opinion about the Revered One?"

"He's a Big One."

"No. He's more. I'd call him a seer. A seer who can pull off miracles. Do you get what I say? Just rolling beedis won't do. You need something in the head to understand all this."

Usan Pillai put down the beedi tray. He looked at Lebbai with new interest.

"I am a disciple of the Revered One. The Revered One made me promise that I'll not talk about it in public till he had left our village. Now that the Revered One has left, I am letting this out before you."

Usan Pillai showed ready enthusiasm in lending an ear to Lebbai's secret. He removed his glasses and stuck them into a bin of coriander seeds.

"Mudalali hurt the feelings of the Revered One and see, the results are already at hand. The man who married Mudalali's daughter is a madman. Such is his power. One should never cross the wishes of a seer."

"You're right, Elebbe."

Usan Pillai was all attention. His habitually busy hands now lay quiet, wedged between his thighs. Lebbai went on.

"Once, from the neighbouring Puvagam a father brought a bewitched daughter. I was there that day. The man brought with him an egg."

" 'What's that?', the Revered One had wanted to know.

" 'An egg,' the man replied.

"The Revered One looked at the egg, turning it this side and that.

" 'Where is the hen that laid this egg?'

" 'I don't know,' the man said. 'This had been buried in the backyard of my house. My daughter was perfectly alright. Somebody has cast an evil spell and buried this egg.'

" 'I must have the hen that laid this egg,' said the Revered One.

" 'How can I possibly find that out,' asked the man helplessly, falling silent.

"'Why don't you answer me?' thundered the Revered One.

" 'What can I say? How could I know?'

" 'You will know.'

"The Revered One kept the egg in his hand and closed his eyes. He opened them in a while.

" 'Oho. She is cooking it in a pot in his kitchen.' He again shut his eyes and opened them. He bade all to do likewise.

"I closed my eyes and opened them as he ordered. By god the Creator! What a strange sight! A hen stood before us.

" 'Crow,' he ordered it.

"Strange are His powers! The hen crowed. He made a hen come alive from the cooking pot and it crowed too."

"Lebbai actually saw that? A hen crowed, did you say?" Usan Pillai found it unbelievable.

"By the God who created me and gave me these two eyes. I didn't tell anyone earlier because of my promise that I won't talk about his visit there."

"Suppose you had let it out?"

"My tongue wouldn't dare."

"True enough."

"Something else happened that I almost forgot to tell. Yesterday I had dozed off in the mosque. Around 2 o'clock in the night someone dressed in a long coat, pajamas and a topi woke me up. It was the Revered One.

"He greeted me with a salam which I returned.

" 'I shall present myself every Friday night and Monday night. You clean up the front room of your house. I won't however be visible to anyone. I shall come even after my death. Whoever comes to me will get the right reward.

" 'How am I know about your presence', I asked him.

" 'There will be the smell of sandal'. That was the last thing I heard. Immediately after, he faded from my sight."

"Praise be upon the Lord. So Lebbai actually saw the Revered One?"

"Not only that. He forbade me to cut any more chickens and told me to hand over my knife to a proper believer who does his worship with faith."

Lebbai took out the knife. "Usan Pillai, keep this."

Usan Pillai found his hands and took out a towel from beneath the seat. He put it on his head.

He extended his two hands and accepted the gift with humility. "Bismillah."

"Put it inside the cashbox. You'll be blessed with plenitude and good name."

Usan Pillai lit a joss stick and waved it into the cashbox. He touched the prized possession to this eyes. He placed it gently inside the box and shut it.

"Lebbai, have a beedi."

Lebbai lit a beedi and instantly got up to go.

"I'll go and clean the room and light a lamp."

"You have to use plenty of water and wash. Shall I come and help?"

"No, no. I can manage it, even at this age, thanks to the Revered One's generosity of spirit." Lebbai walked straight home puffing out curls of smoke.

22

Pattuma's relations were overjoyed to see her pregnant after ten years of marriage, and were thankful to the Revered One and his miraculous powers. They decided to have a bangle ceremony to celebrate the event. The family was all ears to hear the helpless wails of a new-born and the soft patter of a baby's feet. Maimoon, their neighbour, who had walked home along the coast from Maidalam happened to mention to them about the Revered One's visits to Hasanar Lebbai's house on Monday and Friday evenings. Pattumma was beside herself with joy—she had been silently grieving the sudden departure of the Revered One all these days. She bent down, wanting to kiss her belly but had to content herself running her hand over it. Every now and then her eyes wore a distant look as she savoured those electric moments—when she had run her fingers on the Revered One's hirsute chest.

She had been too upset when he had left, with neither a kind glance nor a word that she could cherish as her own. But not anymore. A deep excitement and a pleasurable anticipation coloured her every action. Her fingers kept smoothing her hair for the umpeenth time. Her eyes darted towards the mirror as she bit into her lips and saw them redden.

"Shall we visit the Revered One's mosque?" she asked her mother on a Sunday.

"Why not? Tomorrow is Monday, when the Revered One will appear. We shall go."

Pattumma bathed herself. She combed and wound her hair into a parrot-beak bun. She wore a red lungi and put on a green blouse. She wound an upper cloth with a zari border around her chest and with one end covered her head. She draped the other end loosely on her belly.

Early in the morning mother and daughter reached the jetty and got into a boat. They squatted in a corner, covering their faces with their umbrellas to avoid the glances of the diver community bathing in the river in their loin-cloths. As the boat reached Mulli, they could hear the evening prayer call floating from the River Mosque. As the fish jumped about in the placid waters, Pattumma felt something move within her in a similar fashion. Would the Revered One ever know of it? Will her eyes ever behold him once more? Will he recall those wondrous moments? What will his eyes tell her? Will they hold out mischief? Will he spare her a smile...?

"Dear Creator. Do reveal the Revered One to my eyes," she prayed to herself.

The boat touched the bank. Folding their umbrellas, they walked straight towards the Revered One's mosque which was quite a distance from the jetty. The fragrance of joss sticks wafted through the air as they approached the mosque.

A number of men and women made their way to the mosque. The miracles performed by the Revered One—of putting life into a hen that was in the cooking pot, of making it crow, and of the madness afflicting Mudalali's son-in-law—the stories spread, ripple-like, from village to village. The number of devotees increased by the day.

A big number had already occupied the coloured mats spread outside the Revered One's mosque.

"We shall visit the place again after you deliver. We should have the naming ceremony performed here. If it is a male child we shall name him after the Revered One." Pattumma shook inwardly to hear her mother's words. What? The Revered One's name if it happens to be a male child? No, never.

"If it happens to be a girl we'll call her Beemattai," she told her mother.

"If it's boy?" The mother persisted.

"We won't give it the Revered One's name."

"Are you entirely without gratitude? It should be his name. And don't forget that you are pregnant only because of his powers."

"It won't be his name."

The mother observed the daughter with curiosity. The daughter bent down her head. The two walked silently and sat down in a corner. Everyone assembled there was either uttering silent prayers or moving their prayer beads.

Sandal had been rubbed on the doors and windows. A green cloth had been spread on which was placed a metal lamp. A metal pot, its mouth covered with a piece of green cloth was placed next to it, into which people put their dontations. The mosque opened only on Mondays and Fridays from evening to night. But a few devotees could be seen about the place even on the closed days. Only coconut oil was used to burn the lamp. A special instruction—"Devotees must pour only coconut oil for the lamp: Managing Committee"—was displayed clearly in black and white above the vessel especially provided for those who had pledged oil as offering. In return Lebbai would dip a finger tip into the lamp oil and rub it in the donor's palm, which in turn would be licked by the devotee. A few would be blessed with some joss-stick ash or a few faded jasmine flowers.

Pattumma and her mother stayed there till the night-time prayers. Pattumma was sure that the Revered One would be visible to her. She peered into the room with its dark corners that couldn't be reached by the dull light of the oil lamp. No, the Revered One couldn't be seen. She felt exhausted.

She got up to go. The mother put a few coins into the donation pot and bade the daughter to do likewise. Pattumma was hesitant—did she too have to do that? He would bless her, wouldn't he, whether or not she did that?

For her mother's sake, she put her share of money into the donation pot.

Lebbai gave them a pinch of ash and a few flowers which they received reverentially with both hands.

"Put it into your mouth, daughter."

"Later."

"Must I? And if I don't? Well, I won't. He paid no heed to my entreaties, never showed himself," she thought sorrowfully. Quietly she tied Lebbai's offerings in one corner of her upper cloth.

★ ★ ★

The prayer calls were no longer being heard punctually. The tank was never full; the mats were dotted with lizard droppings. Mudalali sent for Hasanar Lebbai.

"Are you still in this world or not?"

"What do you mean by keeping silent?"

"Had some work."

"What work?"

"Something personal."

"Very well then. Do it all the time. You may leave your job in the mosque." Mudalali was surprised to see an unruffled Lebbai.

Mudalali screamed, "Get out this minute."

"Very well."

No more do I need that job. There's plenty to do in the Revered One's mosque. And earnings that have belied my wildest hopes. The crowds improve by the day. And when the Revered One dies, the crowds will swell, without a doubt. My creator, send him to his grave early. No longer am I a modin, Lebbai thought to himself as he walked briskly. I should stitch myself new clothes, buy a new cap. I should wear only a green scarf on my shoulder.

A green flag with a crescent moon began to flutter on a pole that very day, along with a new board that proclaimed "Masjidul Syedna Muhammad Mustafa Imbichi Koya, the Revered One."

23

Mahmood's daughter was married off amidst a social boycott. Neither the khateeb nor the modin dared to attend the marriage. The marriage register of the mosque did not record the event. But nothing could perturb Mahmood.

"Is the register required on the Day of Judgment?" he asked openly. None could offer a reply.

It was a village custom to inform Mudalali about a wedding a week before. "What's the dowry?" he would ask.

The weight of gold ornaments exchanged and the land gifts, with the Survey number, taluk and the precise location had to be conveyed to him.

Mudalali would listen to everything with an apparently perfunctory interest. He would then demand a donation of ten panams for the mosque.

It had to be handed over respectfully. An invitation too had to be extended to Mudalali. No receipt was, however, given for the donation.

Mahmood did not inform Mudalali of the impending marriage nor of the date. Neither did he invite him and offer money to the mosque.

It was "Baby Goat," the modin who'd been appointed in the place of Hasanar Lebbai, who informed Mudalali of the marriage a day before the event.

"Is that so?"

"Yes."

"What about the donation?"

"I thought he may have given it to you."

"No. You needn't go to slaughter the goat."

"As you wish."

"Nor need the barber community cut it up. Or their women 'do' the bride."

"As you wish."

"And tell everyone about it."

"I shall."

Mudalali's hard decisions upset "Baby Goat" modin and he felt drained of all energy. He sat on the edge of an empty shop massaging his shanks.

He could hardly bear to have to miss the meat dish that would be served at the marriage feast. He felt a sense of utter loss as he thought of the cash gift that could have been his, were he to sacrifice the animal. His hand stroked his chin as he contemplated the losses.

Nobody knew of the name he had been given by his parents after duly uttering Allah's praise into his ears. But everyone knew Baby Goat modin. It was Kannur Musaliyar who had given him this second, more lasting name.

Baby Goat had been working as a modin at the Enayampalli madrasa which was run by Kannur Musaliyar.

Thirty days had passed after the modin's father's death. "When is the Khatam fatiha?" the whole village wanted to know.

"It will be done." He promised one and all.

"It should be done before the fortieth day or I'll suffer a terrible loss of face. Unless I borrow I can't afford to buy meat for the feast," modin thought long and hard but to no avail. When he went to the garden behind the mosque to dry his clothes he spotted a black goat with white spots, innocently grazing.

"Should I or should I not?" The father's death ceremony loomed large before him. Modin made up his mind.

He plucked a few jackfruit leaves to tempt the goat. He tied it with a rope in a secluded spot. He quietly awaited the approach of night and it finally arrived, black as the goat.

Tying the animal's feet he hoisted it on his shoulder. His wife was curious.

"What drama is this now?"

"Your mother's drama. Get away from here. The animal is lame. So I'm carrying him from the market."

"But I heard you calling the faithful for the evening prayer."

"That wasn't me. That was Mammad."

"But it was your voice."

"That's what's great about me. Anyone may call from the place where I call, but everyone will hear only my voice. And tomorrow is my father's khatam ceremony."

"You brought no vegetables from the market?"

"There was no vegetable in the market where I bought this goat."

"A market without vegetables? Strange."

"Look here, woman. You keep on with your questions and I'll hit you on your under-belly."

Early next morning he slit the animal's throat. He skinned it, cut it into pieces all by himself. It was only then that he summoned the cook. He called four or five neighbours and Kannur Musaliyar as well. Even as the feast was on a man came running. He lifted the skin of the dead animal for all to see.

"Hey, modin. What is this business of performing your father's Khatam with my goat? Tell me, now."

The modin laughed.

"Come, join us. Have some rice."

It was after this incident that Kannur Musaliyar called him "Baby Goat" modin.

Mahmood requested him to perform the sacrifice at his daughter's marriage. "Baby Goat" gave him a sad look. "Mudalali has hit one where it hurts most—in the stomach."

"What's the matter?"

"Mudalali has decreed that nobody will visit your house to slaughter the animal."

"Indeed."

"The khateeb will not conduct the marriage."

"I see."

"The barber woman will not come either, to 'do' the bride's face."

"So let that be. My daughter will yet be married off."

"Don't be angry with me. It's Mudalali's dictate. As for me, I lose my little gift and good food as well."

"I'll take care of it."

"Why don't you apologize to Mudalali? We'll both come, the khateeb and I."

"But what is my fault, that I must apologize to him?"

"What about the donation to the mosque?"

"Has he ever rendered accounts of such donations before the village?"

"Allah! Mudalali? Render accounts? Isn't it a sin to ask that of him?"

"What's the greater sin? To ask for accounts? Or to steal public money for personal ends? Modin—what's so special about these Mudalalis? Do they have horns on their heads?"

The news spread in the village that Mudalali had not been invited. Mahmood was duly pronounced an offender and everyone was certain that he deserved punishment. The general consensus was that he should be given forty whip lashes after the Friday sermon. Then they recalled the occasion when Mahmood had brandished a knife at Vappu and got away without as much as a scratch on his body. It was decided that they would get trained toughs from Pundurai to overpower Mahmood. A cry arose, that quickly caught on: "The infidels' school in Mahmood's land should be burnt down."

None attended the marriage except for a couple of close relations.

"Is this a marriage at all, with neither guest nor a register?" His wife was distraught as she hit herself on the forehead.

Mahmood sharpened the knife and checked it for sharpness before slaughtering the goat. "Let us see whether this is acceptable to God or not." He bent down.

"Wait!"

Mahmood straightened his back. It was Hasanar Lebbai.

"Allow me."

Blood gushed out of the animal's slit throat. It beat its hooves in desperation before it quietened down once and for all.

The bridegroom and his family arrived. The former was made to sit on a zari-woven mat. His face shone in the light of the oil lamp. Mahmood did not fail to notice the air of silence in the demeanour of the new relations although he pretended not to notice it.

The bridegroom's father called Mahmood and conveyed to him in low tones: "If the khateeb does not present himself and arrange to have the marriage registered, the marriage won't take place."

"Indeed?"

"Indeed."

Mahmood was a picture of calm. His eyes betrayed nothing but peace, as he held back a thousand conflicting thoughts with all the resoluteness he was capable of. His countenance offered a stark contrast to that of the visitors. He laid a friendly arm on the father's shoulder.

"Please do not misunderstand me. I brought up my children treading the hot sands day and night, and perspiring blood. My children are my very life. I decided to part with one, to entrust her to your son. I shall be only too happy if the marriage is cancelled because of a lack of a wedding register or a khateeb. Now, what's your final verdict?"

"We'll leave with our son."

"By all means."

"Come, my son," the father told the groom.

"You may all leave. But I shall not leave without marrying this girl," the bridegroom spoke in clear tones.

"You cannot, if you are my son."

"I am my father's son. And hence I shall marry this girl, as per his given word."

"Fine. Do so. But you won't step inside my house any more." The father and the rest of the retinue parted.

"My son. I need no one here. I shall myself pronounce my daughter your wedded wife."

24

Whenever the event surfaced in his memory with its attendant train—no invitation, no donation, no registration, no khateeb and no Lebbai—Mudalali was unnerved by the storm it created inside him. He would walk slowly towards his favourite chair, his hands feeling for the walls all the while for support. For hours together he would remain silent with eyes shut.

It was a deliberate attitude that was meant to convey his utter disinterest towards the happenings that went on around him even as he violently suppressed and stifled a scalding anger.

The pretense could however not hold when his daughter's sobs assaulted his ears. They reverberated inside his head in an unending wail and shook him to the core. Nor did anyone quite believe that Mudalali was unaffected by the turn of events.

"Am I being put to test? Did my ancestors too face such a predicament? If they hadn't, well, they were blessed ones. Why do I have to encounter so much? Why was it my lot to witness my sister's youthful dreams fade before they could be even remotely touched by life? Why do I see only tears in the eyes of my only child—eyes that always danced with dreams? The power and prestige of a family that had weathered so many storms needs today but a gust of wind to throw it off-keel. Are my utterances hollow, without power? Are these arms of mine mere appendages, devoid of strength to enforce? Not a voice would dare make itself heard in my presence in the past. And today? A voice rises and it challenges. Is it a lone voice? Or is it a voice goaded by a strong enemy?

"I did not approve of setting up a school here. And so, what do I see instead? A school, challenging my opinion. That is the first affront to my dignity. And I was publicly insulted before a Friday congregation when Mahmood brazenly took out a knife and defied my orders. I thought I would set him right by impeding his daughter's marriage. But the bridegroom decided to stand by Mahmoood and here too it was I who suffered a total loss of face. Wasn't Hasanar Lebbai throwing a challenge when he decided to slaughter the animal for Mahmood? They are all bracing up for war and it is quite possible that they have the support of Western House Mudalali. He must be questing for revenge after I got the latrine constructed opposite his main entrance. And surely he would like his to be the decisive voice in the village."

Well, whatever it might be, he, Ahamadu Kannu Mudalali, wasn't going to give in. He would sell every grove he had if it came to that, but none who was out to defy him would be spared.

"Avukkare!" Mudalali's loud voice echoed through the silent Northern House. It cast fear into the mind of Avukkar who had all the while been leaning against a pillar with nothing to do. It shook the goldsmith who hadn't made any ornaments for the family in recent days. So did Meenakshi who had busied herself picking nits from her hair as there was no paddy to be pounded.

Avukkar appeared before Mudalali.

"Don't waste even a minute and be quick about it. Bring Karuppan."

It was almost dark and Avukkar ran to fetch Karuppan with a hurricane lamp in hand. Karuppan's house was quite far and one reached it after walking an uneven terrain that led through tapioca fields, palm tree groves and hillocks. It wasn't easy to wake up Karuppan once he went off to sleep, drunk up to his nostrils. If he wasn't asleep he would be mouthing obscenities at somebody under the influence of alcohol.

Farid poured oil into the chain lamp as the sun was about to set. As he turned to go, he felt his uncle's eyes riveted on him. He was all attention, at once.

"Did you set aside some hay for the cow?"
"I did."
"Has it been tied up?"
"Yes."

Mudalali asked nothing after that. He went into the inner quarters. As he walked across the passage where the wooden store lay, he couldn't help glancing to the right; his daughter, her hair dishevelled, lay on the cot, her face away from him. With an effort he controlled his emotions.

"Daughter."

There wasn't any response.

"It is sunset. Don't lie down now."

Silence.

Mudalali bent his head down and walked away. He knew that his words weren't heard.

Hearing footsteps behind her, Noohu Pattuma turned her head. She was seated on the prayer mat.

"Did you ask Ayesha?"
"Yes."
"Doesn't she want to go to her in-laws?"
"She won't go."
"Isn't that bad for our prestige?"
"I've told her all that."

"What's so bad about the boy being mad? It's a good family. A family that gifted a crown, no less, to the Venad Maharaja. They've plenty of property, an Arabian horse and a palanquin."

"I've told her everything." Noohu Pattummal continued with reticence. "Brother, it's true they have everything. But the woman in her refuses to be convinced of their worth."

Mudalali did not fail to infer a few things from his sister's tone. He turned back, masking his face with a blank look of incomprehension and reached the mirror hall, taking care this time not to look in the direction of his daughter's room. The flame in the hanging lamp was being teased by the breeze. But Farid had to re-light the lamp again, taking it inside, as the breeze had put out the flame. In the open lot on the Southern side, one could hear a tinkling bell from the stable. It wasn't possible to see the top of the mango tree any longer as night had already descended on it like a thick dark carpet. Mudalali walked to and fro in the verandah and looked at the wall-clock every now or so.

Presently there was a knock on the grand wooden door that had been carved by craftsmen who had worked for the King. Farid opened the door, to encounter Avukkar and Karuppan.

Karuppan removed the cloth that lay on his shoulder and tied it around his waist. He stepped into the courtyard and put his hands together before Mudalali in a gesture of obeisance.

"Avukkar Pillai. You may go."

"Yes."

Karuppan placed one hand on the mouth and placed the other in the chest, his demeanour conveying utter humility.

"Karuppa. Why have you closed your mouth?"

"My precious master. I was too tired. I drank some today."

"Follow me," Mudalali walked towards the open lot, with Karuppan in tow. Farid who'd watched his uncle walking towards the open lot, placed a lamp on the Southern Verandah. Mudalali plucked a leaf off the mango tree and rolled it.

"Do you know why I sent for you?"

"I won't repeat it, if I know."

"Not even your ears will know of it."

"Yes, my Mudalali."

"You can drink upto your nose."

"Not necessary."

"You must. I'll reward you well."

"No."

"I insist. And you must accept it."

"Mudalali is truly a good soul."

"Buy a bottle of kerosene and a matchbox."

"Okay."

"Burn it up."

"Burn what up?"

"You mean you don't understand?"

"No."

"I mean the Englees School."

"Mudalali," Karuppan's tone was dull and disinterested. "It's a temple of Saraswati."

"I am not bothered. And it is Northern House Mudalali who is bidding you to do it."

"I did everything that Mudalali ordered."

"I remember and I'm grateful. Do this now."

"No. I killed when Mudalali told me to. I stabbed when I was told to. I thrashed anyone that Mudalali bade me to. Not once did I disobey. But I refuse to do this."

"You must do this."

"I am an ignorant brute and a cruel man. I know that. But I shall not destroy this Saraswati temple which is going to show light to our children."

"You won't?" Mudalali's voice held out a threat.

"I know only too well that you'll have me beaten and killed by hired men. Good. For all my sins that I committed at your bidding, my body ought to rot away to death. If a quick death can be mine, I shall consider myself lucky."

"You will not burn it?"

"Forgive me."

"You won't?"

Karuppan stood silent.

"You're drunk. Go now."

"Yes. But I do know what's right and wrong." Karuppan did not move.

"Don't stand. Go."

Karuppan was hesitant.

Mudalali walked away in a huff. Karuppan moved away with tentative steps, scratching his head.

Mudalali walked towards the elephant-legged chair and settled down into it.

Karuppan too was deserting him.

"Am I alone? Am I being pushed into a corner? No. I refuse to be pushed. I am no weak man. Yes, I shall put it to torch myself. I need nobody's help," Mudalali stamped his feet and got up in a trice from his chair.

25

The door on the southern side of Ayesha's room led to the well. Someone tapped on the door, once, twice. Ayesha sat up. It had to be Farid. But she was reluctant to open the door.

"Ayesha." She heard a faint voice. Ayesha came near the window. "Who's it?"

"It's me."

She opened the door noiselessly. Farid's eyes were ringed with sadness. As Ayesha attempted to raise the wick of the night lamp, he forbade her.

"But there is no light."

"It will do. Why do we need more light?"

The two gazed at each other.

"Why hasn't Machan shaved?" Ayesha broke the silence.

"Why didn't you live with our new son-in-law?"

"That's a story in itself."

"My story is a sequel to that story."

Ayesha sat down. "Machan, sit down."

"No. I'll stand. I think it was wrong of me to have knocked on your door in the middle of the night."

"I don't think it's wrong. Why didn't Machan sleep?"

"Well, I just can't."

"Why?"

"Because you stay awake."

"I do sleep."

"You lie! Every night I hear your sighs."

"That's ordained by fate."

Silence reigned for a few minutes as neither spoke. Farid gazed at her. His eyes took in her hands and feet, still red with henna. Strong emotions assailed him, causing him physical pain in the region of his heart and his fingers clutched hard at the door. His throat ached as he battled with the violent sobs that threatened to break out. His eyes struggled to hold back the tears.

"Ayesha." Her ears filled with the sound of a heart in pain. She removed the cloth that veiled her face and watched her cousin turn his face the other way. She came near him.

"Why do you weep?"

"I am not weeping."

"What are you thinking about?" She now observed him closely. The face that showed itself to Farid was utterly pale, with eyes that bespoke of irredeemable sorrow.

"You won't go to the son-in-law's house?"

"No." The voice held out a note of finality

"Suppose he were to become alright?"

"I can't live with him."

"Then. . . ?"

"I shall spend the rest of my life alone."

"That's wrong."

"I don't agree with you. Better to be alone than lead a life that the heart doesn't consent to."

"You must be patient."

"Why?" Her voice revealed an eagerness.

"I am going away."

"Where to?"

"Somewhere. Anywhere. I am quite tired of cleaning the cowshed and drawing water."

"So where is Machan going?"

"To Colombo."

"Shall I come too?"

"No. You're another's wife."

Ayesha's face fell. Farid went on.

"I'll come back one day. With fragrant soaps and bundles of cloth. For uncle, I shall bring a belt and an umbrella."

What about me, Ayesha wanted to ask but didn't. She was somebody's wife.

"I'll never forget dear Ayesha. Every moment in Colombo it's her I'll be thinking of."

"Why? I am another's wife."

"Do forgive me. I shouldn't have said that."

"No, you aren't wrong."

"I shall take leave of you now. I shall go away when it's time for the dawn prayer. I haven't told Uncle or Mother. Ayesha can tell them after I've left."

"Machan. You were such a support to me."

"I shall come back. Don't weep." Farid wiped his eyes and left her. Ayesha shut the door behind him and flung herself on the bed. Sobs racked her body.

The cool morning breeze wafted in, carrying the muffled sounds of the early morning prayer call. "I shall go away. . . ." She recalled Farid's words and got up with a start. She opened the door and looked in the direction of the entrance.

Presently she heard the sound of the door opening followed by her father's heavy voice. "Who is it?"

"It's me, Farid."

"Where are you going, so early?"

"To pray."

"Since when did you begin praying in the mosque?"

"Today is the first day."

"Be back early, after you pray."

Tears fell freely from Farid's eyes as he shut the door behind him. "Ayesha, it's for you that I begin this long journey—a journey through the ocean waves." Farid walked away briskly in the dark.

26

Mudalali's eyes felt heavy with sleep. He had kept awake the whole night. He decided to have a bath in cold water before the sun became harsh.

He called out to Farid to fill up the brass vessel. He got no reply. He called again, this time in a louder voice. There was no reply. He got up from the chair in a huff. A slight movement occured at the curtain. It was Noohu Pattuma, her eyes red with crying.

"What is it?"

"He's left us."

"Who?"

"Farid. To Colombo."

"When?"

"This morning, at dawn. He told only Ayesha about it."

"He too has left me?" He returned to his chair.

"Why did you call out to him?"

"Just like that." He lit a cheroot and watched the smoke going up to the elaborately painted ceiling. Soon an unpleasant odour took over the spot.

Mudalali was tiring visibly, day after day. He hardly ventured out of his house and avoided people. The affairs of the mosque interested him no more. He imprisoned himself at home, his peace of mind irretrievably destroyed.

The day dawned as usual. But Mirasa did not come to milk the cows. Nor did Rayappan who cleaned the stable and the cowshed. Mudalali walked into the open field. The mango tree had shed its yellowed leaves all around. This was the very spot to which Karuppan had been summoned on more than one occasion for orders to carry out heinous deeds.

Now even Karuppan despised him. One lost wealth and thereby power too. A thin film of perspiration sprang on his forehead and glistened in the morning sun.

The stable was full of dung and left-over feed. The neigh of that noble animal—there had been none to beat its wind-like speed even on sand—was a wail. For four generations that stable had retained a horse. How could one bear to see it bereft of one? It was all that was left to save the family's honour—the horse and the palanquin.

"The horse and the Karachi buffaloes will stay right where they were, in the Northern House, and till they die. I may lose everything but not the horse. In the time of Ahamadu Kannu Mudalali the horse was sold to another family—I could never submit myself to this insult. I won't allow tomorrow's generations to mock at me."

As Mudalali returned he found Avukkar waiting for him in the front yard.

"You're early. What is it?"

"Today we unsheathed the coconut kernels. All our better trees have been sold. These coconuts have nothing inside them. We can't even pay the labourers with these."

Mudalali recalled his father's days, when the nuts had formed a hill. Ten to twenty men would busy themselves day and night ripping off the outer fibre. When the nuts were loaded on the carts one lost count of them. Such had been the plenitude of the Northern House—it subjected itself to neither counting nor conjecture. And today there wasn't enough to pay the labour. Shame.

"The coconut trader wants his money. And we have no money to pay him."

"Pledge the next crop."

"He won't agree."

"So?"

"As I said yesterday, the horse and the carriage. . . ."

"Avukkaru!" A cry of distress rose from Mudalali's throat. "There hasn't been a day when the Northern House had an empty shed. No upstart new rich man will use the horse and carriage in which the Northern House Mudalali rode. Make over a plantation or even two plantations."

"Once you do that, you have nothing left to eat."

"I and my family can starve to death if there is no income. But I shall not remain indebted. Settle it through the registrar tomorrow."

Avukkar sank into deeper and deeper gloom with each sale of Mudalali's plantations. He had begun to work for the family at the age of eight. Now he was sixty-four. His spare skeletal body and the blood coursing through the veins under the skin owed their all to that family. It was sorrowful to have to see the relentless fall of that mighty house. It was his fervent wish that till his end he should get his last morsel from what that family could spare him.

Avukkar turned away to do his master's bidding.

Mudalali sat down in his favourite chair. Steam rose from the hot tea that his wife had served in a china bowl. As he spotted the barber, he recalled that it was a Friday. After submitting himself to a shave and a tonsure, he reached the well. Noohu Pattuma came out running.

"Let me draw water."

Mudalali gave her the rope. Finishing his bath, he once more settled down in the chair. The clock on the wall showed half past eleven. There was still time for the sermon. He expected the modin to come to him a little later. As he leaned and closed his eyes a thousand images flitted across.

A faceless woman's turmeric-stained hands came forth around his neck. As he gasped, his limbs thrashed about uncontrollably. His eyes popped out and his tongue lolled.

"Save me. My Martyrs of Badr." Mudalali woke up with a scream and looked all around him. The women of the house and the labour working in the coconut dump came running to him.

"What is it?"

"Nothing. It was a dream."

The clock showed three. Soon it would be time for the evening prayer. Everybody must be waiting for him for the sermon. The modin might have come and gone away, too afraid to disturb him. He ought to be coming now, to escort him to the Friday prayer.

Mudalali wore a laundered lungi and put on a muslin vest and a collarless shirt. He fixed the ivory buttons and tied a turban with a length of special voile manufactured by the Ratnamala company. He rubbed a fragrant essence on his shirt and turban. He awaited the modin's arrival; his eyes repeatedly went back to the clock. As the hands showed half past four, the wafting breeze brought in the faint sounds of the evening prayer call.

"Allahu Akbar!" It shook Mudalali. Today the noon prayer had taken place without him, without his knowledge. He looked at the sky to ensure that the sun wasn't setting in the east. No. It wasn't.

The ground beneath him gave way. He and the chair on which he sat fell deeper and deeper, in an endless fall. Even the bull which balanced the earth between its horns wasn't to be seen. Had it been sighted, he could have at least stopped the fall by clutching at its horns.

27

The crowd that had assembled in the old mosque was united in its verdict that it was the new "Englees man" teacher who had made Mahmood swerve from the right path. The verdict echoed and reechoed at Usan Pillai's shop and Asan's chukku neer shop. It was the teacher rather than Mahmood who was the object of their intense dislike. For it was he who was out to make infidels of them. First it was Mahmood's son. And now, through the son, the father. The boy freely roamed around in knickers, revealing his knees. Usan Pillai had even actually seen Mahmood buying it in the Wednesday market.

"Mahmood. Is this permissible?"

"Absolutely so." Mahmood was decisive. Usan Pillai did not say anything to Mahmood. But he made it a point to talk against the teacher: "The new Englees man is declaring everything permissible."

"Go away, you trouble-maker. It is I who want to see my son in knickers."

As soon as he reached the shop, Usan Pillai passed on the story of Mahmood's costly purchase amounting to three chakkarams into the ever-eager ears of Hasanar Lebbai. The latter spat out noisily.

"Go, I say. Don't even mention him to me. Today he'll buy his son a pair of knickers. Tomorrow he'll have him sent to the barber's shop to get his hair cropped. All these are but signs of the end."

The Friday congregation busied itself with the topic of the new school and the teacher as soon as the prayer was over. It was unequivocally decided that the teacher was no more than a lackey Englees man out to mislead the good folk. He was using Mahmood and Mahmood was being backed by Western House Mudalali.

As he finished calling out the faithful for the noon prayer, Baby Goat modin stepped out of the mosque as usual, to call the Northern House Mudalali.

"Going far, are you?" Mahmood's voice rang out loud. A few men, turning round the prayer beads and counting God's praises on their fingers, turned to look.

"I am off to fetch Mudalali."

"You needn't."

Mahmood spoke out clearly. "Those who hear the call and present themselves at the mosque may pray. Those who don't, needn't." The crowd was shocked.

"But ... but...."

"But what? If he doesn't turn up, will this mosque come down? Or will the prayers we offer become tainted? You need nobody's permission to pray here."

"Is it anywhere stated in a book that the prayers should await the arrival of Northern House Mudalali?" Western House Mudalali flung the question towards the modin as he finished counting and reverentially put the beads to his lips.

As Baby Goat modin groped for a reply, Mahmood went on relentlessly, "Is he spending from his pocket for the oil lamp? Or for modin's wages?"

The modin put his hands on his chest, "My Creator!"

"Modin. Come back and stay put. If he wants to come, he will come. At exactly quarter past one, we shall pray." Western House Mudalali's voice held a note of firmness.

"If you think that Northern House Mudalali's presence is obligatory, the sermon of the forthcoming Friday will take place at the water-front mosque east of the Memorial rock," Mahmood warned.

Modin washed his feet and entered the mosque.

"It wasn't your father or mine that constructed this mosque. It was raised by Malik Ibn ud-Dinar. And the village foots the bills of the mosque."

The crowd lent Mahmood a sullen acquiescence. The absence of Mudalali nagged many, though they were tamed into silence by Mahmood's forceful words.

"It's quarter past one," reminded Mahmood. The khateeb, suitably dressed in a long coat, got up on the pulpit. He received the ceremonial sword with utmost reverence from modin. Supporting himself with it he greeted the congregation, "Peace be upon you."

At forty minutes past one, the prayer finished. Nobody spoke as Mahmood left the mosque. No sooner was he out that voices rang out.

After the noon prayers, Baby Goat modin walked straight towards the Northern House. As he pushed open the door and saw a sleeping Mudalali he squatted right there. Hours sped by and Mudalali showed no signs of waking up. He got up, and stood with the sun behind him. As he measured the shadow with his feet, the modin knew he had to return to the mosque for the evening prayer. As soon as the prayer was over, he was back in the Northern House.

He was fear-stricken and Mudalali's incensed eyes stopped his heartbeats. His face was white as a sheet of paper.

"Come." It was like the voice of one willing to commit murder.

Modin placed one tentative step forward.

"Where does the sun rise?"

"In the east."

"Sets where?"

"In the west."

"That was true till yesterday. From today the directions are reversed."

"It's no fault of mine."

"Yes. I know. I know it all."

"I was coming to call you."

"Mahmood stopped you. I know that. But Northern House Mudalali isn't one to give up. Next Friday I shall pray at the Midalam mosque. In my father's day a man from the eastern side of the Memorial rock wouldn't even dare to walk on the western side. Times have changed. Today his voice is being heard in the mosque. Never will I step into it for a Friday congregation."

"It was no mistake of mine."

"You may leave. From now the Western House fellow or Mahmood will pay your wages."

Mudalali awaited the approach of night. His mind was littered with thoughts—inchoate, unstrung, relentless. A family that depended on him. Income that had been reduced to a trickle. The black ink stain retained by his left thumb; the moment it was pressed on white paper, the plantations went over to someone else. Plantation number 2639—measuring an acre and ten cents, with its immense yield of coconut—had once belonged to Kochu Pirai Maimoon. The grove lay on Mudalali's palanquin route. The trees with their thick crowns had often led him to enquire of their owner.

One day he had heard a woman's voice, while riding the palanquin: "Ahamadu Kannu."

The insolence of the caller sent waves of shock through him. A woman had dared to call him by name. The palanquin was ordered to be put down and men despatched to trace the offender.

"It is Kochupirai Maimoon," Mudalali was informed.

"Why did you call me by name in the middle of road?"

"I did not do so."

"Whose name is it then?"

"My son's."

"So your son sports my name?"

"Yes."

"Don't you know that none in the village can have the same name as I?"

"No."

"Where are you from?"

"Kulachai. He was born there and named there."

"It is an offence, nonetheless, wherever you might have named him. To have called out my name within my earshot is your second offence."

"Do be forgiving, my Mudalali. My son was eager to see your palanquin. It was to show it that I called him."

"Your crimes cannot be pardoned. As punishment you will make over plantation number 2639 measuring one acre and ten cents to me by legal deed. The registrar will come to your house tomorrow. You will do as I said."

"I am a widow, my Mudalali. I have young daughter at home. I have no other means. Please forgive me this once."

"No."

Tears had streamed down her eyes as her left thumb pressed the paper in front of the registrar. She fell down unconscious the next moment. That was the last plantation that Mudalali had parted with.

The entire house had fallen asleep. Mudalali got up and lowered the wick of the night lamp. He picked up his six-cell torch and noiselessly walked towards the main entrance. He stared at the dark as though challenging it. His legs felt a little stiff but he did not lose heart. Far away, a night fowl announced the midnight hour. A rat jumped and ran near his feet.

The torch was firmly stuck in his armpit. A white cat crossed the way. Mudalali ignored everything and walked with determined steps into the depths of darkness—towards where the Englees school stood.

28

Days of relentless sun. A box of a room that could not be visited by breeze or light. Mehboob Khan and Nur Jehan spent the months in utter discomfort.

Once the room was shut—it had no door but a wooden plank that fitted into grooves—it was totally dark. An oil lamp had to be kept glowing even in the afternoon to drive out the darkness.

Nur Jehan instinctively knew the time of her husband's arrival for the midday meal. He would tap thrice on the plank with his knuckle and she would remove the plank from within.

It was late in the evening when he returned that day. He had been busy tackling a difficult problem—low attendance. Out of the enrolled twenty-one, only eight or nine children came to school.

Were there to be a marriage or death, not even one child would be visible in the school. Nor on days when there would be a good haul from the sea. Mehboob Khan could then be seen looking out into the street, his cane stuck between side and forearm.

Even when the children wouldn't actually present themselves, they would be "present" within the little boxes in the columns of the register. The records had always to be there for the inspector could visit any time. Today was one such day when Mehboob Khan had ensured that he was ready for such an event.

The dusk prayer call could be heard as he reached home. The heat was beyond endurance. His body was bathed in sweat.

He wiped his face and body with a towel and remarked, "Another six months inside this box and we'll be dead."

"At last you spare a thought to it. I had told you long back that the room won't suit us."

"Where else could we go?"

"I can no longer stand it. Please take me home."

"If you do that, I shall die of hunger. This place does not have even a decent tea shop."

"Then why don't you seek a transfer? Why stick to this place?"

"If I put in a request I shall certainly get it. But that will mean that the children of this village will remain illiterate. This society is destroying itself, feeding on fake pride. The poor are swindled and exploited to the bone by the rich. If any change is to occur in the state of affairs, it has to be through education. And I must do my mite to that end. Even if you go home I shall live by myself, all alone."

Nur Jehan chose to remain quiet.

The call for the night prayer broke out of Baby Goat modin's throat. Mehboob Khan spread out a mat and lay down. Nur Jehan lowered the flame and did the same.

Mehboob Khan was unable to sleep. He reflected on the spiders building webs across the dimly lit ceiling. So were these men who began and ended their lives inside a trap of ignorance, like human worms. They were wedged between the sharp nails of landlords who squeezed their life-blood. Lives that were spent in mortal fear of their cruel commands, that were like piercing arrows! Human non-animals that baked like bricks in a kiln, a torturous heat draining them atom by atom!

One could almost physically hear the moments being chewn between the jaws of the midnight hour. Dogs barked.

Nur Jehan was in deep sleep. Mehboob Khan lay sleepless. His mind was crowded with thoughts and more thoughts, like a widespread banyan tree.

A sudden noise made him shake with fear. He sharpened his ears. A shower of stones hit the roof. He got up and woke Nur Jehan quietly. "Be quiet. Someone's throwing stones on the roof."

Nur Jehan huddled close to her husband, her eyes wide with fright as Mehboob Khan increased the flame in the lamp. For a while all was quiet.

Again stones rained, this time on the entrance plank.

Nur Jehan hugged her husband and sobbed. "Don't. All this is a test. It is neither a witch nor a spirit. It's the villagers."

The stones continued to rain. Mehboob Khan's patience broke. "Who is it?"

A few shuffling feet could be heard. Mehboob Khan came out and asked Nur Jehan for the lamp. Stones littered the yard. A small gust of wind from a branch of the jackfruit tree stifled the flame. He got back into the room.

He hugged his wife who was shaking with fright.

"I want to go home."

"I'll send you."

"They'll kill you."

"I came with an aim. If I die for it, it's good for me."

Nur Jehan sobbed her heart out at her husband's words.

Mehboob Khan sat through the night on his haunches his arms encircling his knees.

Baby Goat modin climbed the platform of the Old Mosque and opened his mouth wide, putting a finger into each ear. The prayer call emerged from his throat and floated by in the quiet dawn hour.

Only Asan's shop would be open at that hour. Till eight in the morning, one could get hot tea and puttu. Mehboob Khan decided to buy himself some tea and get rid of the fatigue. As he stepped out, his foot touched something slimy. A pungent smell hit the roof of his head. Closing his nostrils, he asked his wife for the lamp. The dim light showed blobs of human excrement dotting the entire front yard. There was nowhere that he could plant his feet safely on the ground.

Mehboob Khan broke down. Why was this his lot? He wiped his eyes secretly, without Nur Jehan's knowledge.

He washed his feet and got into the room, waiting for the sun to rise.

29

"Syedna Muhammad Mustafa Imbichi Koya the Revered One is no more," Hasanar Pillai informed Usan Pillai who promptly spread the news.

"How did Elebbe come to know?" asked the villagers who came to mourn the Revered Ones' death.

"Through a vision. Seers are like that. They don't die. They disappear. That's their death. They later appear in visions and inform us that they have died."

The villagers were sorrowful at the passing away of the Revered One. They recalled his great deeds. "A good man. A man with immense powers. A great soul who put life into a hen that was already in the cooking pot and made it crow too."

Hasanar Lebbai appeared to be in deep sorrow. Tears poured from his eyes every now and then. He needed to be consoled frequently.

Soon crowds swelled in the new mosque of the Revered One. A few saw him in their dreams. Soon after they would be seen in the mosque reciting the Sura Yasin and making offerings. The donation pot rapidly filled up with money and gold. Animals pledged to the mosque as offerings were auctioned off.

Hasanar Lebbai's cheeks filled out. Eyes that used to be sunk into pits were now visible and shone. He was always well-dressed. He wore a green shawl around his shirt and tied a turban as well. Sandals adorned his feet.

The devotees gathered in the Revered One's mosque offered special prayers for the collapse and ruin of the "Englees" school. Donations were put into the pot specially to that effect. Hasanar Lebbai consoled them: "With the power of your prayers I shall knock down that `Englees' school of that son of a bitch."

"Ameen!" A few hands stroked the donation pot and then put them to the eyes.

"First, he should be driven out. Then his school."

That night Hasanar Lebbai met "Dirty Innard" Hanifa and "Big Belly" Mammaseen. He whispered in their ears: "At night you should throw stones on his roof. He'll run for his life, thinking that it's the devil's work. You clear your bowels in his front yard. He'll really know his place."

"Agreed. But that's only if we get our fill of fish and tapioca. So Lebbai, spare us some of the silvery stuff."

"Indeed! Aren't you satisfied with the plenitude that the Revered One has cast around you?"

"Won't do for us."

With supreme reluctance Lebbai extracted two eight chakkaram pieces. "Hold this, my enemies. This should fill your stomachs."

Silence reigned all around the Northern House. No one talked much. Laughter was like a permanently stilled wave. A bare minimum of words passed for conversation. The silence was broken at times by the sound of the kitchen vessels and the mewing black cart, prowling on the boundary or near the rat-trap.

Mudalali's voice could hardly be heard, even inside the house, leave alone the street. Avukkar had nothing to do but to lean against a pillar and yawn, seated near his master. Mudalali no longer chewed betel. He lit cheroot after cheroot and threw them about, hot and glowing like the thoughts that occupied him.

Ayesha chose to imprison herself in her room. She would constantly to lie on her stomach, face down. She would dream of Farid, his talking eyes and gentle smile, his pearl-like teeth. Every nerve in her youthful body became taut, making her pray to God that they did not snap. She grew afraid even of her dreams and the nights that brought them.

She recalled a story that her mother's elder sister had told her, when she was a child—the story of a beauty who in her dream fell in love with a jinn. She would recall it quite well after all these years.

Once upon a time there was a king. He prayed and pledged all sorts of offerings to God to be blessed with a girl-child. At last his wish was fulfilled. A flood of happiness engulfed the royal family. Food was distributed to the poor. Dancers and singers were summoned to the palace.

The princess wasn't ever allowed to place her bare feet on the ground. She was brought up with much affection and pampering.

The fame of her beauty spread to every corner. Numerous kings and emperors proposed marriage to her. But she would accept nobody's suit.

The princess would often dream of handsome young men and finally fell in love with one. His extraordinary looks made her swoon. She longed to see him appear in broad daylight. Deep in her heart she vowed that she should somehow see him when she was awake.

One night, as she was sleeping, she was woken up by the sound of something tapping on the window. She opened it.

What a surprise! It was the youth. She forgot her very being in a surge of happiness. She let open the door. A full moon had bloomed in the sky.

"Come, my love. Let us walk in the flower garden," the handsome youth said. The princess followed him.

"Do you see the milky moon?"

"Yes."

"Isn't it a night of intoxication?"

"True."

Both walked. They crossed the garden and reached the sea shore.

"Do you feel the sand, how fine it is?"

"I do."

"Dearest. Even sand tingles to the touch of your feet."

"No, it tingles to yours." They both laughed. She covered her face with her hands and shyly saw her lover's moustache.

"Where is your country?"
"Across the sea."
"Take me with you."
"Dearest, you cannot reach there."
"Who are you?"
"I am the prince of a land that is across the sea."
"I shall come with you."
"Dearest, if you wish to do that you will have to mother my child."
"I shall."

The sand grains thrilled to the touch of their bodies. The moon hid his face behind a veil.

Aunt stopped the story.

"Aunt, who was it that captivated the princess?"

"A jinn."

"Did she go to the jinn's land?"

"No. The following day the King sent his soldiers to search for the princess. One of them found her lying lifeless on the sea shore."

A flood tears had flowed from Ayesha's eyes at the sad end of the princess.

Ayesha opened the window to let in some air. She sat erect on her haunches to avoid the recurring dreams.

A faint noise could be heard at the main entrance. She peeped from the window and saw a figure come in. She held her breath till the figure approached closer to the mild light cast by the night lamp. She let out her breath only when the figure was well within the front yard.

"Father! At the dead of night where did he have to go? Where is he coming back from?"

She thought hard but could find no answer.

Father came to the well and washed his hands and feet. He let out a tired long breath, tightened the lungi around his waist, and went back to the elephant-legged chair.

A little later she smelt smoke in the air. The same smell that emerged when they burnt dry coconut fronds to heat water. As moments slipped by, the smell became more acrid. At a far distance the sky reddened. Soon the sound of men running helter-skelter could be heard.

"Fire. A terrible fire."

Her heart fluttered. Her mother and aunt woke up. Ayesha opened the door and ran to her aunt.

She hugged her. "Fire. There's a fire."

Viyattuma lengthened the wick of the brass lamp that was in the middle quarter. She ran to her husband.

"There is a fire."

"Go in. In the last days of creation these are ordained to happen," Mudalali shouted. He shut his eyes and lay in the chair, the face showing not even the slightest change of expression.

30

The day broke on a terror-stricken village. The red rays of the rising sun scared the men, as their minds were filled with the picture of flames reaching out to the sky. The red sun was for the moment one more fire in a round shape.

Nobody had seen such a fire earlier. The sound of the bamboos splitting in the flames had made a few unconscious. Their very lives seemed to be snuffing out as the green fronds burned.

They neither washed nor cleaned themselves as the sun peeped from behind Elephant Rock like a blood-drunk denizen. They gathered around the smoking ruins of the Englees school. The sight evoked tentative smiles of satisfaction, not deterred by their unclean teeth.

Hasanar Lebbai strolled in, sandals resounding, hands folded behind the back. A string of prayer beads continued to slip through between his fingers.

"Last night having been a Thursday night I sought the blessings of the Revered One. I got the reply forthwith. He let loose the jinns that caused the fire," Hasanar Lebbai declared with pride.

The crowd surrounded him. Lebbai instantly rose an inch inside his sandals. He puffed his chest.

"Was the fire not the act of a man?" someone asked.

"Is there so bold a man?"

Nobody answered. They stared at the challenging eyes of Lebbai whose brows stayed arched for a while.

"It is the wrath of God Himself. The mumbo-jumbo of the Third Book fellows cannot sell here. The fire that destroyed came straight from the hell-fires." Lebbai turned back and walked, sandals resounding. Prayer beads continued to slip between his fingers.

None noticed Mehboob Khan who sat alone underneath a coconut tree. Tears steaked his cheeks and he muttered to himself like a man deranged.

The crowd was in a festive mood. Even a speck of ash flying in the wind became a source of joy.

They all believed that the Revered One had commanded the jinns to destroy the infidel reading-place with fire brought from Hell itself. More men began to believe in his powers than ever before. Their village was indeed fortunate to have been trod by his austere feet. And without doubt he was a true seer.

Hasanar Lebbai's popularity soared to a peak. There could be no two opinions that he was a true disciple of the Revered One. All the villagers, young and old, stood up in reverence at the very sound of his sandals. Lebbai would tilt his head and cast a proud glance at them. The very glance was perceived to hold a strange power.

It was only Mudalali who didn't deign to care for Lebbai, about which the Lebbai said and merely once: "He'll come around. He has to. Let's see how long he stays away from casting his dues into this donation pot."

Mudalali never visited the mosque of the Revered One. Nor did he venture into changing his opinion of Lebbai. "Well do I know the Hasanar Pillai with his bug-stained collarless shirt that stank of sweat, who earned his five panams like a mute slave. Even better do I know about his Revered One," Mudalali shouted into the empty room, making strange gestures. He did not see Avukkar who had just come to see his master.

Mudalali laughed aloud as though he had heard a joke. The laughter continued and his body shook. Beads of perspiration burnt out on the bald head.

The women rushed to the scene, puzzled by Mudalali's loud laughter and incoherent noises. The sight of a tired Avukkar, weeping silent tears held them behind the curtain. They lifted it slightly to see Mudalali whose mad gesturing continued.

"Who is it, flying on a white horse? Whoever it may be, I refuse to see him," he shouted again as he shut his eyes tight.

The women wept silently, apprehensive and uncomprehending.

"Why do the bunch of you laugh at me? Am I a mad man? I am Aima Kannu Mudalali of the Northern House, don't you know that? Right as far as the eyes can see, everything here belongs to me, everything," Mudalali opened his eyes. The women now began to sob aloud.

The horse beat its hooves in the shed. Tears flowed from its eyes without stop.

Avukkar knew why it was weeping. For want of food. There was no grass. No oil cake to be boiled and fed to the animal. It searched for bits of grass in the dung-heap. It foamed at the mouth. Avukkar could not bear the sight and had walked out of the shed.

"Daughter Ayesha. Look here. Your groom is stepping out of the carriage. Open the door," Mudalali shouted.

Everybody turned to look at the main entrance. All they saw was a mud path whose dust lay settled.

Avukkar's tears flowed freely like an unchecked flood. He got out of the house silently, not uttering a word to anyone. The mud felt cool against his feet. He refused to oblige the curious villagers as he walked along the Puttan river* and on the rocks of the Sheikh's Mosque. He walked through endless fields and plantations, not stopping at all till he reached Raman Vaiddiyan's house. Gasping, he rapped on the door loudly. The door opened.

"There's an illness."

"Who's ill?"

"Mudalali."

Avukkar stood like one seeking alms. Raman Vaiddiyan took his little box that contained pills and the palm-leaf umbrella. He almost ran to keep pace with the swift Avukkar.

By the time they reached the Northern House, it was evening. Mudallai had seated himself in the middle courtyard. It was unswept and full of betel-stained spittle and rubbish.

---

*Earlier referred to as Valiyaru, and as Ananta Marthandam Canal.

"My Mudalali! The Vaiddiyar is here. He's come to the visitor's room."

"This is my house and I shall stay where I please. Who are you to tell me?"

Mudalali directed his wrath at Avukkar, who glared at the Vaiddiyar.

"And who is he?"

"Vaiddiyar."

"Who has fallen ill now?"

"Mudalali has been running a fever. Let the Vaiddiyar check."

"What if I have a fever? You mind your own business."

The Vaiddiyar stood at a distance as Avukkar fell silent, bowing his head. Mudalali addressed Raman Vaiddiyar.

"So you are Tangappan Vaidiyar's son Raman Vaiddiyar?"

"Yes."

"Sit."

Vaiddiyar sat down near Mudalali.

"Why did you come?"

"I was told that you have a fever."

"Do I? Check." Mudalali extended his arm. Vaiddiyar felt Mudalali's wrists. He then tapped his fingers gently on the floor.

"Have I a fever?"

"Yes." He got up to talk to Avukkar. "For forty days you have to give him a decoction."

"Yes."

"For forty days herbal water should he poured on his head and a paste of lentils applied."

"What's the ailment?"

"Can't you make out? Madness." The sobs of the women could be openly heard behind the curtain.

Vaiddiyar sat down to make a list of the necessary items for the patient's treatment.

"Daughter Ayesha. Your husband has arrived in the horse carriage. Open the door." The words sounded like a lament as Mudalali walked to and fro in the yard.

31

Avukkar was unable to sleep that night. He did not touch the food that his wife had placed in front of him. He rolled out the mat and lay down silently. He was harsh on the wife who wished to know the reason for his gloom.

His mind was full of the Northern House horse and Mudalali. He kept thinking of the animal's thin neck and its wet, grief-stricken eyes. His ears were crowded with Mudalali's noisy behaviour and his constant lament for his daughter. And the horse—that noble animal which had been the crowning glory of the Northern House. It's days were numbered now, just like the unstoppable decline of Ahamadu Kannu Mudalali, once the very fount of pomp and splendour. Eyes that had beheld only authority were now vacant spots of bemusement. Incoherent words tumbled from a mouth that had once uttered nothing but commands.

The night's silence accentuated the roar of the waves. Palm fronds bristled against one another. Avukkar sat up and removed his shirt. His neck was ringed with sweat.

He stepped down to the front yard and gazed at the sky. There was no way of knowing what time it was. How long would it be for the dawn prayer? He gazed at the eastern horizon. The morning star was yet to rise. He cursed the sky that revealed an unredeemed dark and came back to his bed.

The sight of the horse haunted him again. It's sorrowful glance was like a piercing thorn in his mind.

"Mudalali . . . my Mudalali!' Avukkar moaned to himself. He opened the door. But his feet were reluctant to step out into a darkness that was as black as unkempt tresses.

He spat out angrily at the rigidity of the hour that would not let dawn arrive.

"Who is it?" It was his wife.

"It's me."

"Lie down and sleep."

Avukkar returned and sat down on the mat. A firefly flickered across. Or was it a spirit flitting across in the form of fire? Avukkar shut his eyes tight in fear.

The distant sound of the song of the fishermen out for a midnight catch wafted into his ears. He resented that familiar sound for his thoughts about the horse and Mudalali would no longer stay rooted. He waited avidly for Baby Goat modin's prayer call. One wasn't allowed to get out before the prayer call, for it was the hour when spirits prowled. Their feet could be tied down only by the sound of the call.

How long did the night stretch? Only sleep had the capacity to swallow it whole. When one lay sleepless, one knew not how long it stretched.

Could the horse be sleeping? What of Mudalali?

At last the prayer call was sounded, after what had been an unbearable wait.

Avukkar opened the door and stepped out. The morning star twinkled in the eastern sky. Swift as an arrow, he tore through the lingering darkness and reached Mudalali's house.

His hand stretched itself to knock at the entrance door, as always. But the knock wasn't necessary. He could see the fluttering tongue of the flame of the lamp hanging in the verandah as though it was muttering something.

He wondered who it could have been who'd opened the door at that hour. Could it be Mudalali who was no longer in full possession of his senses?

Avukkar panicked to find the reclining chair empty. He searched for his master and at last found him perched on top of the grain-hold in the southern side of the house. Mudalali took no notice of Avukkar and blabbered incoherently. Perhaps he had forgotten to shut the main door. He went towards the open lot now visible in the early morning light and entered the stable.

"Oh, my Maker!" The heart of that loyal servant burst into pieces to see the proud head of the animal stretched straight, legs spread out. Blood had oozed from its mouth.

"I was not fated to give it even a drop of medicine," Avukkar sobbed uncontrollably.

His loud weeping attracted the attention of the women. "What happened?" asked a shocked Viyattuma as she saw Avukkar sobbing like a child.

"My horse is dead." Viyattuma's eyes turned wet.

Avukkar rushed to Mudalali, who was shaking his legs and laughing at something in an invisible dimension. He looked at Avukkar as one would a stranger.

"The horse is dead," with an effort he wrenched the words out of his throat and sobbed.

"Let it," Mudalali sent out a sudden snatch of a laugh.

Avukkar bent his head and wiped his eyes. He clutched at a pillar to steady himself and collapsed on the floor.

Hours passed by, laden with sorrow. The rays of the sun climbing up the outer wall of the kitchen declared that the dawn prayer's hour had passed by. Till that day, the women of the Northern House had not missed a single dawn prayer. Ayesha would as a rule sleep after the others had slept. And she would be the first one to wake up, at the early morning hour. That had been her routine ever since she returned from her husband's home.

Today, she didn't seem at all to be affected by the turmoil in the house following the horse's death. The previous night too she had been extraordinarily silent and had declined food.

"Daughter." Noohu Pattuma called out as she knocked at the door. The door opened at her touch to reveal an empty room. She shouted her name aloud. The whole house was searched.

The women began to wail in fright. Avukkar ran across to them. "Ayeshamma is not to be seen." Avukkar was stunned. He hit himself hard on the forehead and searched every nook and cranny. He climbed the lofts and peered several times in the well.

"Ayeshamma is missing." Viyattuma told her husband who continued to sit on top of the grain-hold. Her words conveyed nothing to him. The stream of nonsensical babble was punctuated by sudden bursts of laugher; it continued, almost interminably. It ended in a question: "What? Ayeshamma is missing?" He kept shaking his legs, comprehending nothing.

32

Ayesha grew thinner with each passing day. Her eyes were no more like twin poems. Roses were no longer in bloom on her cheeks. The moist petals of her lips were now dry.

Her mind could take root nowhere and she was trapped in a tangled skin of restless thoughts. She could stand none in her room and particularly resented her near ones. She hated her Father and Mother more than anyone else. They seemed so distant, totally alien. Life was to her nothing but unredeemed darkness with a rough terrain to tread on.

Ayesha felt like one serving a life-term in a dungeon—a deranged father, a home that was perishing before her very eyes, a family that depended on a mad man for its head.

Enough! Enough of it all!

The woman in her had longed silently and for a long time—for that love, that touch, which alone would lend complete meaning to her womanhood. But she had lost, despite the patient wait. Her womanhood had but to scald itself in the white-heat of her emotions. It was as if all doors to fulfillment were shut and were being knocked at only to announce mournful news.

No longer was it of use to reach for what would never be hers. No avenues were open to her. No need to live in a society that was numb and blind to the plight of a young woman and denied youth its due.

The sound of the nets being dragged floated in from the seashore accompanied by the refrain of the fishermen. She was filled with memories of the sea and the backwaters.

Rushing waves that rose, roared, frothed and panicked toward the shore, wetting her feet. Touching her silver anklets, the water drenched her skirt that she had taken care to hitch up. Mother had caned her for that. Father had intervened and wiped her tears. She had sobbed the whole day and well into evening.

It was the last Wednesday of the year. After an oil massage and bath, one drank the holy water into which had been mixed magical chants written with charcoal on a china plate. It ensured that she was obsolved of all sins committed till that day. Each year one did that on the last Wednesday and earned Allah's forgiveness.

On one such Wednesday she had been to the river, prancing all the way, holding Father's finger. How curious it was to see rotting coconut husk being beaten into golden lengths of fibre, on the river bank.

"What's this, father?"

"That's how coir is made."

It was even more fascinating to see the fibre being wound through a wheel and twisted into coir.

She sighted a small building on top of a rock. "Whose house is that?"

"It's not a house. It's a mosque. Nagur Shakhul Hamid Auliya once visited it."

Father had taught her so much that day. Standing on the rock she had watched the water. And the sheer immensity of it. Baby-sized waves. Playful little fish. At a distance two rocks rose above the water.

"Father. Shall we go there?"

"No, no. Never. Chettichi, the sea-devil, lives right below them. She drags people coming to bathe in the river by winding her tresses around the legs and takes them down below into a huge sea. And below that rock is the pathway to the Sasta temple."

The very mention of the sea-devil had terrified her. Their maid Khadija had already told her about the sea-devil killing the man who had gone to bathe alone in the river during the hour of the Friday congregation.

Her existence was that of a prisoner locked in the same room, month after month. The mind had no longer the strength to push away each dawning day. Never could she hope to be an object of anyone's love and affection. And her volatile emotions might egg her on to deeds that a heartless society could never forgive.

Was hers not a bleak existence, barren and lonely, like a wild wayside tree? Of what use was a body that could never feel the pleasurable kick of a life growing in its womb?

Ill-fated! She was ill-fated!

Ayesha opened the door. The dark seemed to have fanned out from the netherworld below. She quietly unlatched the entrance door. She prayed fervently that no one might see her as she decided to take the short cut to the left of the Old Mosque to the River Mosque. On one side of the path was the barber settlement, with a pond nearby. The huge rock there provided a cover for people who eased themselves on their way to the river for a bath. Dogs would prowl there day and night.

They shouldn't bark now, giving her away. Then the barbers might wake up and discover her.

When she was attending Hasanar Lebbai's madrasa, years ago, she would frequent the spot in search of unripe dates. The barber woman Nafisa complained to her Mother. "Dear, the child has grown long in arm and limb. Her breast is also swelling. Should she be plucking dates near the rock?"

Mother had beaten her till she was black and blue. No more did she venture there for fruit.

Ayesha glanced in the direction of the rock. No dogs were in sight. Or did she seem to them devoid of life?

She was now near the river. She went up the rocky steps. The clock inside the mosque ticked away, loud, unhindered. The waves seemed to utter deep secrets. The rushing river hit hard against the sides of the rock. The water's sharp slaps made the night all the more cruel.

Watching the event were the rising minarets and the platform from where the faithful were hailed.

She was the last link in a chain of five generations of proud might. She turned back to look. She could feel a strange tremor imploding in the still mosque. Was it the spirit of Nagur Shakhul Hamid Waliullah, who had enjoyed this breeze a hundred years ago, bidding her to retrace her steps?

That holy man would know her heart's torment—how it tossed, turned, burned and shriveled up. He would never extend his unseen arms to pull her back from her destiny.

A thousand stars winked in the sky and sprayed their light to reveal the river. She could see the two jutting rocks. And between them the long tresses of the sea-devil spread out wide on the entire river. Someone was beckoning her to the very spot.

As she turned back to the see the mosque for the last time, her eyes turned moist. She thought of Father. And Mother, and Mami, whose youth too had turned into ash. Their horse, the symbol of their family pride. The elephant-legged chair. Hasanar Lebbai who'd carry Father's turban and sandals to represent Father's consent to the Friday congregation.

"Machan. Do forgive me. Now we'll never meet again. Don't trouble yourself to sail on a ship from Colombo to reach me. I am leaving you. I am fated to. Forgive me, Machan; we'll be united in death."

She plunged into the fierce flow. The water rose up with an eerie sound in the four directions and splashed. She went down, came up again. Her limbs thrashed about in water. For a while her body bobbed up and down. It then floated away.

Valiyaru presented the usual spectacle of its swift course to carry out its tryst with the sea, its secret well-hidden within it.

Glossary

Aliph	: First letter of the Arabic alphabet
Aliph Lam Meem	: First line of the first chapter of the Koran
Allahu Akbar	: "God is the greatest"
Audubillah	: "I seek refuge in God (from Satan)"
Auliya	: "Favourite of God"; a person of spiritual attainment
Ayatul Kursi	: A verse from the second chapter of the Koran; recited before sleeping or when afraid to ensure safety of one's self and the environs
Bismillah	: "In the name of God"
chakkarams	: Currency of the erstwhile Travancore State; a denomination higher to kasu
chittirai	: First month of the Tamil new year (Mid-April—Mid-May)
chukku neer	: a hot decoction of dry ginger and molasses
Eid (Id)	: The most important Muslim festival celebrated after a month of fasting and prayers
elelam	: A fishermen's song that uses the word as a refrain
Erabbe	: Corruption of the word Lebbai
fajr	: Dawn prayers
Fourth Book	: A reference to the Koran; the preceding three books being the Taurat (Torah) Zabur (Book of Psalms) and Injil (Gospel)
Iblis	: Shaitan or Satan
isha	: Night prayers
kafir	: One who does not follow Islam; more precisely, an atheist
kanji	: rice gruel
kasu	: The erstwhile Travancore state's currency constituting the lowest denomination
khatam fatiha	: Prayers for a deceased person, followed by a feast

khateeb	: The person who recites the sermon or khutba
khus	: A fragrant and cooling herb
khutba	: The sermon delivered before the noon prayers on Fridays and on special occasions such as Eid
kissa	: Story or legend in the oral tradition
lungi	: A length of cloth stitched at the ends and worn simply by tying around and tucking in at the waist
madrasa	: A school for imparting religious education
maulood	: Songs of praise devoted to the Prophets
maulavi	: A person highly trained in Islamic law; also, a teacher
minbar	: The pulpit from which the sermon is recited
modin(ar)	: The muezzin, the person, who issues the calls to prayer or the azaan
momin	: A muslim
ottappams	: Pancakes made of egg and powdered rice
panam	: The erstwhile Travancore state's currency; a higher denomination than chakkarams
puttu	: A steamed dish of powdered rice blended with coconut; of dry texture
Rabi-ul-Aval	: "The first spring month"; third month of the Islamic calender
roti	: unleavened bread made of wheat or maize flour
Shaban	: The eighth month of the Islamic calender
Subhanallah	: "Glory of God."
sunnat	: Additional prayers offered before the prescribed prayers
Sura-e-Yasin	: Thirty-sixth chapter of the Koran, containing verses on the Last Day
surma	: A greyish-black powder used to line eyes
talli	: Thread or gold chain worn around the neck by a married woman, customarily worn by Tamil women
Tehsildar	: Head of a tehsil, an administrative unit, with authority to collect land revenue
zuhar	: Afternoon prayers